# everyday

# pasta

This edition published in 2010
LOVE FOOD is an imprint of Parragon Books Ltd

Parragon
Queen Street House
4 Queen Street
Bath BA1 1HE, UK

Copyright © Parragon Books Ltd 2007

LOVE FOOD and the accompanying heart device is a registered trade mark of Parragon Books Ltd in Australia, the UK, USA, India and the EU.

ISBN: 978-1-4054-9397-0

Printed in China

Designed by Terry Jeavons & Company

Notes for the Reader
This book uses both metric and imperial measurements. Follow the same units of measurement throughout; do not mix metric and imperial. All spoon measurements are level: teaspoons are assumed to be 5 ml, and tablespoons are assumed to be 15 ml. Unless otherwise stated, milk is assumed to be full fat, eggs and individual vegetables are medium, and pepper is freshly ground black pepper.

The times given are an approximate guide only. Preparation times differ according to the techniques used by different people and the cooking times may also vary from those given. Optional ingredients, variations or serving suggestions have not been included in the calculations.

Recipes using raw or very lightly cooked eggs should be avoided by infants, the elderly, pregnant women, convalescents and anyone suffering from an illness. Pregnant and breastfeeding women are advised to avoid eating peanuts and peanut products. Sufferers from nut allergies should be aware that some of the ready-made ingredients used in the recipes in this book may contain nuts. Always check the packaging before use.

Vegetarians should be aware that some of the ready-prepared ingredients used in the recipes in this book may contain animal products. Always check the packaging before use.

# everyday
# pasta

# introduction

Where would we be without pasta? It has to be the most useful invention ever – it is delicious, inexpensive, nutritious, quick and easy to cook, very satisfying and incredibly versatile. The fact that it

comes in so many shapes and sizes makes it even more interesting, as well as fun to eat for adults and children alike.

The shape you use is largely a matter of choice, and you have about 200 different shapes to choose from! There are, of course, a few classic combinations. Spaghetti, for example, is the one to serve with meatballs or a rich, meaty, bolognese sauce – if you want to be both well fed and entertained, look out for the really long

variety of spaghetti, which is quite a challenge to eat! Macaroni & Cheese simply wouldn't be the same made with any other shape of pasta, and Fettuccine Alfredo has a ring to the name that pasta lovers know well!

Pasta is almost foolproof to cook, but it's worth noting one or two points. Firstly, always bring the cooking water to a rapid boil before adding the pasta. Once the pasta is in the pan, adjust the heat so that the pasta cooks at a steady boil without boiling over. The most important thing to remember is not to overcook the pasta. 'Al dente' means 'still firm when bitten' and this is what you need to aim for – eating limp, soggy pasta is quite an unpleasant experience! Follow the recommended cooking time in the recipe or on the packet and keep tasting toward the end of the time to make sure you get it just right – or you can, of course, follow the Italian tradition of throwing a test piece at the wall and if it sticks, you'll know it's done!

Making your own fresh pasta is surprisingly easy and there are a few recipes for you to try. For everyday use, though, fill your store cupboards with a good variety of pasta shapes, select your favourite dishes and make the most of this treasure of an ingredient.

# soups & salads

Adding pasta to a soup adds an extra texture and 'bite'. Look out for packets of special soup pasta shapes, which are small and cook in almost no time, or use fine vermicelli, broken into pieces. The classic Italian pasta soup is Minestrone, which is packed with vegetables and beans and is ideal as a substantial lunch or supper dish, served with fresh crusty bread. Brown Lentil & Pasta Soup, Italian Chicken Soup, Fish Soup with Anellini and Genoese Vegetable Soup are also full of protein and very satisfying. Blending pesto sauce into a soup makes it rich and delicious, or use it as a topping, French-style, in Vegetable & Bean Soup.

Pasta salads are just fabulous, and you can really make the most of all the creative shapes that are available. As the name implies, ear-shaped pasta goes into Orecchietti Salad with Pears & Blue Cheese, a gorgeous blend of flavours and textures. Pasta Salad with Nuts & Gorgonzola uses farfalle, little bow shapes that go particularly well in salads, and fusilli tricolore – pasta spirals in plain, spinach, and tomato flavours to represent the colours of the Italian flag – goes into Pasta Niçoise, a twist on the classic French salad which looks beautiful and would make a stunning centrepiece for an alfresco summer lunch. It tastes quite wonderful, too!

# minestrone

## ingredients

**SERVES 6**

2 tbsp olive oil

55 g/2 oz rindless pancetta or
    lean bacon, diced

2 onions, sliced

2 garlic cloves, finely chopped

3 carrots, chopped

2 celery stalks, chopped

225 g/8 oz dried cannellini
    beans, soaked overnight in
    cold water to cover

400 g/14 oz canned chopped
    tomatoes

2 litres/64 fl oz beef stock

350 g/12 oz potatoes, diced

175 g/6 oz dried pepe
    bucato, macaroni or
    other soup pasta shapes

175 g/6 oz green beans, sliced

115 g/4 oz fresh or frozen
    peas

225 g/8 oz savoy cabbage,
    shredded

3 tbsp chopped fresh flat-leaf
    parsley

salt and pepper

fresh Parmesan cheese
    shavings, to serve

## method

**1** Heat the olive oil in a large, heavy-based saucepan. Add the pancetta, onions and garlic and cook, stirring occasionally, for 5 minutes.

**2** Add the carrots and celery and cook, stirring occasionally, for a further 5 minutes, or until all the vegetables are softened.

**3** Drain the soaked beans and add them to the pan with the tomatoes and their can juices and the beef stock. Bring to the boil, then reduce the heat, cover and simmer for 1 hour.

**4** Add the potatoes, re-cover, and cook for 15 minutes, then add the pasta, green beans, peas, cabbage and parsley. Cover and cook for a further 15 minutes, or until all the vegetables are tender. Season with salt and pepper. Ladle the soup into warmed soup bowls and serve immediately with Parmesan cheese shavings.

# potato & pesto soup

## ingredients

### SERVES 4

3 slices rindless, smoked,
    fatty bacon or pancetta
450 g/1 lb floury potatoes
450 g/1 lb onions
2 tbsp olive oil
625 ml/20 fl oz chicken stock
625 ml/20 fl oz milk
100 g/3$\frac{1}{2}$ oz dried conchigliette
150 ml/5 fl oz double cream
chopped fresh parsley
salt and pepper
garlic bread and Parmesan
    cheese shavings, to serve

### pesto sauce

55 g/2 oz finely chopped
    fresh parsley
2 garlic cloves, crushed
55 g/2 oz pine nuts, crushed
2 tbsp chopped fresh basil
    leaves
55 g/2 oz freshly grated
    Parmesan cheese
white pepper
150 ml/5 fl oz olive oil

## method

**1** To make the pesto sauce, put all of the ingredients in a blender or food processor and process for 2 minutes, or blend by hand using a mortar and pestle.

**2** Finely chop the bacon, potatoes and onions. Cook the bacon in a large saucepan over medium heat for 4 minutes. Add the olive oil, potatoes and onions and cook for 12 minutes, stirring constantly.

**3** Add the stock and milk to the pan, bring to the boil and simmer for 10 minutes. Add the conchigliette and simmer for a further 10–12 minutes.

**4** Blend in the cream and simmer for 5 minutes. Add the chopped parsley, salt and pepper and 2 tablespoons of the pesto sauce. Transfer the soup to individual serving bowls and serve with Parmesan cheese shavings and fresh garlic bread.

# fresh tomato soup

## ingredients

### SERVES 4

1 tbsp olive oil
650 g/1 lb 7 oz plum
    tomatoes
1 onion, cut into quarters
1 garlic clove, sliced thinly
1 celery stalk, chopped
    coarsely
500 ml/18 fl oz chicken stock
55 g/2 oz dried anellini or
    other soup pasta
salt and pepper
fresh flat-leaf parsley,
    chopped, to garnish

## method

**1** Pour the olive oil into a large, heavy-based saucepan and add the tomatoes, onion, garlic and celery. Cover and cook over low heat for 45 minutes, occasionally shaking the pan gently, until the mixture is pulpy.

**2** Transfer the mixture to a food processor or blender and process to a smooth purée. Push the purée through a sieve into a clean saucepan.

**3** Add the stock and bring to the boil. Add the pasta, bring back to the boil and cook for 8–10 minutes, until the pasta is tender but still firm to the bite. Season with salt and pepper. Ladle into warmed bowls, sprinkle with the parsley and serve immediately.

# brown lentil & pasta soup

## ingredients

**SERVES 4**

4 slices lean bacon, cut into
    small squares

1 onion, chopped

2 garlic cloves, crushed

2 celery stalks, chopped

50 g/1¾ oz farfalline or
    spaghetti, broken into
    small pieces

400 g/14 oz canned brown
    lentils, drained

1.25 litres/40 fl oz hot
    vegetable stock

2 tbsp chopped fresh mint

fresh mint sprigs, to garnish

## method

**1** Place the bacon in a large frying pan with the onion, garlic and celery. Dry fry for 4–5 minutes, stirring, until the onion is tender and the bacon is just beginning to brown.

**2** Add the pasta to the pan and cook, stirring, for 1 minute to coat the pasta in the fat.

**3** Add the lentils and the stock and bring to the boil. Reduce the heat and simmer for 12–15 minutes, or until the pasta is tender but still firm to the bite.

**4** Remove the pan from the heat and stir in the chopped fresh mint. Transfer the soup to warmed soup bowls, garnish with fresh mint sprigs and serve immediately.

# italian chicken soup

## ingredients

**SERVES 4**

450 g/1 lb skinless, boneless
chicken breast, cut into
thin strips

1.25 litres/40 fl oz chicken
stock

150 ml/5 fl oz double cream

115 g/4 oz dried vermicelli

salt and pepper

1 tbsp cornflour

3 tbsp milk

175 g/6 oz canned sweetcorn
kernels, drained

## method

**1** Place the chicken in a large saucepan and pour in the chicken stock and cream. Bring to the boil, then reduce the heat and simmer for 20 minutes.

**2** Meanwhile, bring a large heavy-based saucepan of lightly salted water to the boil. Add the pasta, return to the boil and cook for 10–12 minutes, or until just tender but still firm to the bite. Drain the pasta well and keep warm.

**3** Season the soup with salt and pepper. Mix the cornflour and milk together until a smooth paste forms, then stir it into the soup. Add the sweetcorn and pasta and heat through. Ladle the soup into warmed soup bowls and serve.

# chicken & pasta broth

## ingredients

**SERVES 6**

350 g/12 oz boneless
    chicken breasts

2 tbsp corn oil

1 onion, diced

250 g/9 oz carrots, diced

250 g/9 oz cauliflower florets

950 ml/28 fl oz chicken stock

2 tsp dried mixed herbs

125 g/4¹/₂ oz dried small
    pasta shapes

salt and pepper

freshly grated Parmesan
    cheese, for sprinkling
    (optional)

fresh crusty bread, to serve

## method

**1** Using a sharp knife, finely dice the chicken, discarding any skin.

**2** Heat the corn oil in a large saucepan and quickly cook the chicken, onion, carrots and cauliflower until they are lightly coloured.

**3** Stir in the chicken stock and dried mixed herbs and bring to the boil.

**4** Add the pasta shapes to the pan and return to the boil. Cover the pan and simmer the broth for 10 minutes, stirring occasionally to prevent the pasta sticking together.

**5** Season the broth with salt and pepper and sprinkle with grated Parmesan cheese, if using. Serve with crusty bread.

# fish soup with anellini

## ingredients

### SERVES 6

2 tbsp olive oil

2 onions, sliced

1 garlic clove, finely chopped

1 litre/32 fl oz fish stock
or water

400 g/14 oz canned chopped
tomatoes

1/4 tsp herbes de Provence

1/4 tsp saffron threads

115 g/4 oz dried anellini

salt and pepper

450 g/1 lb monkfish fillet, cut
into chunks

18 live mussels, scrubbed
and debearded*

225 g/8 oz raw prawns,
shelled and deveined, tails
left on

* discard any damaged
mussels or any that do
not shut immediately
when tapped

## method

**1** Heat the olive oil in a large heavy-based
saucepan. Add the onions and garlic and
cook over low heat, stirring occasionally, for
5 minutes, or until the onions have softened.

**2** Add the fish stock with the tomatoes and
their can juices, herbs, saffron and pasta and
season with salt and pepper. Bring to the boil,
then cover and simmer for 15 minutes.

**3** Add the fish, mussels and prawns. Re-cover
the pan and simmer for a further 5–10
minutes, until the mussels have opened, the
prawns have changed colour, and the fish is
opaque and flakes easily. Discard any mussels
that remain closed. Ladle the soup into
warmed bowls and serve.

# white bean soup

## ingredients

**SERVES 4**

175 g/6 oz dried cannellini
    beans, soaked overnight in
    cold water to cover

1.6 litres/48 fl oz chicken or
    vegetable stock

115 g/4 oz dried spirali

6 tbsp olive oil

2 garlic cloves, finely chopped

4 tbsp chopped fresh flat-leaf
    parsley

salt and pepper

fresh crusty bread, to serve

## method

**1** Drain the soaked beans and place them in a large, heavy-based saucepan. Add the stock and bring to the boil. Partially cover the pan, reduce the heat and simmer for 2 hours, or until tender.

**2** Transfer about half the beans and a little of the stock to a food processor or blender and process to a smooth purée. Return the purée to the pan and stir well to mix. Return the soup to the boil.

**3** Add the pasta to the soup, return to the boil and cook for 10 minutes, or until tender.

**4** Meanwhile, heat 4 tablespoons of the olive oil in a small saucepan. Add the garlic and cook over low heat, stirring frequently, for 4–5 minutes, or until golden. Stir the garlic into the soup and add the parsley. Season with salt and pepper and ladle into warmed soup bowls. Drizzle with the remaining olive oil and serve immediately with crusty bread.

# genoese vegetable soup

## ingredients

**SERVES 8**

200 g/7 oz spinach leaves
225 g/8 oz plum tomatoes
2 onions, sliced
2 carrots, diced
2 celery stalks, sliced
2 potatoes, diced
115 g/4 oz frozen peas
115 g/4 oz green beans, cut
    into 1-inch/2.5-cm lengths
2 courgettes, diced
3 garlic cloves, sliced
4 tbsp olive oil
2 litres/48 fl oz vegetable or
    chicken stock
salt and pepper
140 g/5 oz dried soup pasta
freshly grated Parmesan
    cheese, to serve

### pesto sauce

2 garlic cloves
25 g/1 oz pine nuts
115 g/4 oz fresh basil leaves
salt
55 g/2 oz freshly grated
    Parmesan cheese
125 ml/4 fl oz olive oil

## method

**1** Remove any coarse stalks from the spinach and shred. Peel the tomatoes by cutting a cross in the bottom of each and placing in a heatproof bowl. Cover with boiling water and let stand for 35–45 seconds. Drain and plunge into cold water, then peel. Deseed and dice the tomatoes, then place in a large, heavy-based saucepan together with the onions, carrots, celery, potatoes, peas, beans, courgettes and garlic. Pour in the olive oil and stock and bring to the boil over medium–low heat. Reduce the heat and simmer gently for about 1 1/2 hours.

**2** Meanwhile, make the pesto. Put the garlic, pine nuts, basil and a pinch of salt into a mortar and pound to a paste with a pestle. Transfer the mixture to a bowl and gradually work in the Parmesan cheese, using a wooden spoon, followed by the olive oil, to make a thick, creamy sauce. Taste and adjust the seasoning if necessary. Cover with plastic wrap and chill in the refrigerator until required.

**3** Season the soup and add the pasta. Cook for a further 8–10 minutes, or until the pasta is tender but still firm to the bite. Stir in half the pesto, remove the pan from the heat and let stand for 4 minutes. Taste and add more salt, pepper and pesto if necessary. Ladle into warmed bowls and serve at once. Hand round the freshly grated Parmesan cheese separately.

# vegetable & bean soup

## ingredients

### SERVES 4–6

225 g/8 oz fresh broad beans
2 tbsp olive oil
2 large garlic cloves, crushed
1 large onion, finely chopped
1 celery stalk, finely chopped
1 carrot, peeled and chopped
175 g/6 oz firm new
    potatoes, diced
950 ml/30 fl oz vegetable
    stock
2 beefsteak tomatoes, peeled,
    deseeded and chopped
salt and pepper
1 large bunch of fresh basil,
    tied with kitchen string
200 g/7 oz courgette, diced
200 g/7 oz green beans,
    trimmed and chopped
55 g/2 oz dried vermicelli,
    broken into pieces, or
    small pasta shapes

## pesto sauce

100 g/3$^1$/$_2$ oz fresh basil leaves
2 large garlic cloves
1$^1$/$_2$ tbsp pine nuts
50 ml/2 fl oz fruity extra-virgin
    olive oil
55 g/2 oz finely grated
    Parmesan cheese

## method

**1** If the broad beans are very young and tender, they can be used as they are. If they are older, use a small, sharp knife to slit the gray outer skins, then 'pop' out the green beans.

**2** Heat the olive oil in a large heavy-based saucepan, over medium heat. Add the garlic, onion, celery, and carrot and sauté until the onion is soft, but not brown.

**3** Add the potatoes, stock and tomatoes and season with salt and pepper. Bring the stock to the boil, skimming the surface if necessary, then add the basil. Reduce the heat and cover the pan. simmer for 15 minutes, or until the potatoes are tender.

**4** Meanwhile, make the pesto sauce. Whiz the basil, garlic, and pine nuts in a food processor or blender until a thick paste forms. Add the extra-virgin olive oil and whiz again. Transfer to a bowl and stir in the cheese, then cover and chill until required.

**5** When the potatoes are tender, stir the broad beans, courgette, green beans, and vermicelli into the soup and continue simmering for 10 minutes, or until the vegetables are tender and the pasta is cooked. Taste, and adjust the seasoning if necessary. Remove and discard the bunch of basil.

**6** Ladle the soup into bowls and add a spoonful of pesto sauce to each bowl.

# pasta niçoise

## ingredients

### SERVES 4

115 g/4 oz green beans, cut
  into 2-inch/5-cm lengths

225 g/8 oz dried fusilli tricolore

100 ml/3$^1$/$_2$ fl oz olive oil

2 tuna steaks, about
  350 g/12 oz each

salt and pepper

6 cherry tomatoes, halved

55 g/2 oz black olives,
  pitted and halved

6 canned anchovies,
  drained and chopped

3 tbsp chopped fresh flat-leaf
  parsley

2 tbsp lemon juice

8–10 radicchio leaves

## method

**1** Bring a large, heavy-based saucepan of
lightly salted water to the boil. Add the green
beans, reduce the heat, and cook for 5–6
minutes. Remove with a slotted spoon and
refresh in a bowl of cold water. Drain well. Add
the pasta to the same pan, return to the boil,
and cook for 8–10 minutes, or until tender but
still firm to the bite.

**2** Meanwhile, brush a griddle pan with some of
the olive oil and heat until smoking. Season
the tuna with salt and pepper and brush both
sides with some of the remaining olive oil.
Cook over medium heat for 2 minutes on each
side, or until cooked to your liking, then
remove from the griddle pan and reserve.

**3** Drain the pasta well and tip it into a bowl.
Add the green beans, cherry tomatoes, olives,
anchovies, parsley, lemon juice, and remaining
olive oil and season with salt and pepper. Toss
well and let cool. Remove and discard any skin
from the tuna and slice thickly.

**4** Gently mix the tuna into the pasta salad.
Line a large salad bowl with the radicchio
leaves, spoon in the salad, and serve.

# tuna & herbed fusilli salad

## ingredients

**SERVES 4**

200 g/7 oz dried fusilli

1 red pepper, deseeded
and cut into quarters

150 g/5½ oz asparagus spears

1 red onion, sliced

4 tomatoes, sliced

200 g/7 oz canned tuna in
brine, drained and flaked

### dressing

6 tbsp basil-flavoured oil or
extra-virgin olive oil

3 tbsp white wine vinegar

1 tbsp lime juice

1 tsp mustard

1 tsp honey

4 tbsp chopped fresh basil,
plus extra sprigs to garnish

## method

**1** Bring a large pan of lightly salted water to the boil. Add the pasta, return to the boil, and cook for 8–10 minutes until tender but still firm to the bite.

**2** Meanwhile, put the pepper quarters under a preheated hot grill and cook for 10–12 minutes until the skins begin to blacken. Transfer to a plastic bag, seal and set aside.

**3** Bring a separate pan of water to the boil, add the asparagus, and blanch for 4 minutes. Drain and plunge into cold water, then drain again. Remove the pasta from the heat, drain, and set aside to cool. Remove the pepper quarters from the bag and peel off the skins. Slice the pepper into strips.

**4** To make the dressing, put all the dressing ingredients in a large bowl and stir together well. Add the pasta, pepper strips, asparagus, onion, tomatoes, and tuna. Toss together gently, then divide among serving bowls. Garnish with basil sprigs and serve.

# orecchiette salad
# with pears & blue cheese

## ingredients

**SERVES 4**

250 g/9 oz dried orecchiette

1 head of radicchio,
    torn into pieces

1 oak leaf lettuce,
    torn into pieces

2 pears

3 tbsp lemon juice

250 g/9 oz blue cheese,
    diced

55 g/2 oz chopped walnuts

4 tomatoes, cut into quarters

1 red onion, sliced

1 carrot, grated

8 fresh basil leaves

55 g/2 oz corn salad

4 tbsp olive oil

3 tbsp white wine vinegar

salt and pepper

## method

**1** Bring a large heavy-based saucepan of lightly salted water to the boil. Add the pasta, return to the boil, and cook for 8–10 minutes, or until tender but still firm to the bite. Drain, refresh in a bowl of cold water and drain again.

**2** Place the radicchio and oak leaf lettuce leaves in a large bowl. Halve the pears, remove the cores, and dice the flesh. Toss the diced pear with 1 tablespoon of lemon juice in a small bowl to prevent discolouration. Top the salad with the blue cheese, walnuts, pears, pasta, tomatoes, onion slices, and grated carrot. Add the basil and corn salad.

**3** Mix the remaining lemon juice and the olive oil and vinegar together in a measuring cup, then season with salt and pepper. Pour the dressing over the salad, toss, and serve immediately.

# warm pasta salad

## ingredients

**SERVES 4**

225 g/8 oz dried farfalle or
    other pasta shapes
6 pieces of sun-dried tomato
    in oil, drained and chopped
4 spring onions, chopped
55 g/2 oz rocket, shredded
$1/2$ cucumber, deseeded
    and diced
salt and pepper
2 tbsp freshly grated
    Parmesan cheese

### dressing

4 tbsp olive oil
$1/2$ tsp superfine sugar
1 tbsp white wine vinegar
1 tsp Dijon mustard
salt and pepper
4 fresh basil leaves,
    finely shredded

## method

**1** To make the dressing, whisk the olive oil, sugar, vinegar, and mustard together in a bowl. Season with salt and pepper, then stir in the basil.

**2** Bring a large, heavy-based saucepan of lightly salted water to the boil. Add the pasta, return to the boil, and cook for 8–10 minutes, or until tender but still firm to the bite. Drain and transfer to a salad bowl. Add the dressing and toss well.

**3** Add the chopped sun-dried tomatoes, spring onions, rocket, and cucumber, season with salt and pepper, and toss. Sprinkle with the Parmesan cheese and serve warm.

# italian salad

## ingredients

### SERVES 4

225 g/8 oz dried conchiglie

50 g/1¾ oz pine nuts

350 g/12 oz cherry tomatoes, halved

1 red pepper, deseeded and cut into bite-size chunks

1 red onion, chopped

200 g/7 oz mozzarella di bufala, cut into small pieces

12 black olives, pitted

25 g/1 oz fresh basil leaves

fresh Parmesan cheese shavings, to garnish

### dressing

5 tbsp extra-virgin olive oil

2 tbsp balsamic vinegar

1 tbsp chopped fresh basil

salt and pepper

## method

**1** Bring a large pan of lightly salted water to the boil. Add the pasta, return to the boil, and cook for 8–10 minutes until tender but still firm to the bite. Drain, refresh under cold running water, and drain again. Let cool.

**2** Meanwhile, heat a dry skillet over low heat, add the pine nuts, and cook, shaking the skillet frequently, for 1–2 minutes until lightly toasted. Remove from the heat, transfer to a dish, and let cool.

**3** To make the dressing, put all the ingredients in a small bowl and mix well together. Cover with plastic wrap, and set aside.

**4** To assemble the salad, divide the pasta among 4 serving bowls. Add the pine nuts, tomatoes, pepper, onion, cheese, and olives. Sprinkle over the basil, then drizzle over the dressing. Garnish with Parmesan cheese shavings and serve.

# pasta salad
# with curry dressing

## ingredients

**SERVES 4**

115 g/4 oz dried farfalle

4–5 large lettuce leaves

1 green pepper, deseeded
and chopped

1 red pepper, deseeded
and chopped

2 tbsp chopped fresh chives

115 g/4 oz white mushrooms,
chopped

dressing

2 tsp curry powder

1 tbsp caster sugar

125 ml/4 fl oz corn oil

50 ml/2 fl oz white wine
vinegar

1 tbsp single cream

## method

**1** Bring a large heavy-based saucepan of lightly
salted water to the boil. Add the pasta, return
to the boil and cook for 8–10 minutes, or until
tender but still firm to the bite. Drain, rinse in
a bowl of cold water and drain again.

**2** Line a large bowl with the lettuce leaves and
tip in the pasta. Add the green and red
peppers, chives and mushrooms.

**3** To make the dressing, place the curry
powder and sugar in a small bowl and
gradually stir in the oil, vinegar and cream.
Whisk well and pour the dressing over the
salad. Toss and serve.

# pasta salad with nuts & gorgonzola

## ingredients

**SERVES 4**

225 g/8 oz dried farfalle

2 tbsp walnut oil

4 tbsp safflower oil

2 tbsp balsamic vinegar

salt and pepper

280 g/10 oz mixed salad leaves

225 g/8 oz Gorgonzola
   cheese, diced

115 g/4 oz walnuts, halved
   and toasted

## method

**1** Bring a large, heavy-based saucepan of lightly salted water to the boil. Add the pasta, return to the boil and cook for 8–10 minutes, or until tender but still firm to the bite. Drain, refresh in a bowl of cold water and drain again.

**2** Mix the walnut oil, safflower oil and vinegar together in a measuring cup, whisking well, and season with salt and pepper.

**3** Arrange the salad leaves in a large serving bowl. Top with the pasta, Gorgonzola cheese and walnuts. Pour the dressing over the salad, toss lightly and serve.

# pasta salad with chargrilled peppers

## ingredients

**SERVES 4**

1 red pepper

1 orange pepper

280 g/10 oz dried conchiglie

5 tbsp extra-virgin olive oil

2 tbsp lemon juice

2 tbsp green pesto

1 garlic clove, finely chopped

3 tbsp shredded fresh
   basil leaves

salt and pepper

## method

**1** Preheat the grill. Put the whole peppers on a baking sheet and place under the hot grill, turning frequently, for 15 minutes, or until charred all over. Remove with tongs and place in a bowl. Cover with crumpled kitchen paper and reserve.

**2** Meanwhile, bring a large saucepan of lightly salted water to the boil. Add the pasta, return to the boil and cook for 8–10 minutes, or until tender but still firm to the bite.

**3** Combine the olive oil, lemon juice, pesto and garlic in a bowl, whisking well to mix. Drain the pasta, add it to the pesto mixture while still hot and toss well. Set aside until required.

**4** When the peppers are cool enough to handle, peel off the skins, then cut open and remove the seeds. Chop the flesh coarsely and add to the pasta with the basil. Season with salt and pepper and toss well. Serve.

# meat & poultry

Pasta is useful for making a little meat go a long way! There are some truly delectable meat-based pasta sauces in this section. All devotees of Italian food love Spaghetti & Meatballs, and there is also a recipe for a rather sophisticated Spaghetti Bolognese, another all-time favourite. Two simple yet elegant recipes to try are Spaghetti alla Carbonara and Saffron Linguine – they are both ready to serve in less than fifteen minutes and are dishes to impress guests when you're short of time but big on style. Pasta & Pork in Red Wine Sauce is also very chic, garnished with quail eggs.

If you like a little heat in your pasta sauce, there are plenty of spicy options, including Chilli Pork with Tagliatelle, Rigatoni with Ham, Tomato & Chilli Sauce and Macaroni with Sausage, Pepperoncini & Olives. Spaghetti with Parsley Chicken has a delicious, fresh-tasting sauce with lemon rind and a little fresh root ginger.

If you are keen to have a go at making your own pasta, try Creamy Chicken Ravioli and Chicken Tortellini. Ravioli is very easy, just a matter of spacing out the filling evenly on a sheet of pasta, covering it with a second sheet and cutting out the squares. Tortellini, on the other hand, involves some manual dexterity, but it's great fun to make and once you've mastered it, you will never look back!

# spaghetti & meatballs

## ingredients

### SERVES 2

2 thick slices white bread,
    crusts removed

2 tbsp olive oil

1 red onion, chopped

2 garlic cloves, finely chopped

400 g/14 oz canned chopped
    tomatoes

8 basil leaves

2 tbsp tomato purée

1 tsp sugar

salt and pepper

450 g/1 lb minced beef

2 eggs

1 tbsp chopped fresh parsley

1 tbsp chopped fresh basil

350 g/12 oz dried spaghetti

freshly grated Parmesan
    cheese, to serve

## method

**1** Place the bread in a shallow bowl and add just enough water to cover. Soak for 5 minutes, then drain and squeeze the bread to remove all the liquid.

**2** Heat the oil in a saucepan, add the onion and half the garlic and cook over medium heat, stirring occasionally, for 5 minutes. Add the tomatoes with their juice, basil leaves, tomato purée and sugar and season with salt and pepper. Bring to the boil, reduce the heat and simmer, stirring occasionally, for 20 minutes until thickened and pulpy.

**3** Mix the bread, beef, eggs, remaining herbs, garlic and $1/2$ tsp of salt by hand in a large mixing bowl. Roll small pieces of the meat mixture into balls. Drop the meatballs into the tomato sauce, cover the pan and cook over medium heat for 30 minutes.

**4** Meanwhile, cook the spaghetti in a saucepan of lightly salted boiling water for 10 minutes, or until tender but still firm to the bite. Drain well.

**5** Transfer the spaghetti to a large shallow serving bowl. Arrange the meatballs and sauce on top. Sprinkle 2 tablespoons of freshly grated Parmesan cheese over the top and serve with more cheese in a bowl on the side.

# spaghetti bolognese

## ingredients

**SERVES 4**

2 tbsp olive oil

1 tbsp butter

1 small onion, finely chopped

1 carrot, finely chopped

1 celery stalk, finely chopped

50 g/1³/₄ oz mushrooms, diced

225 g/8 oz minced beef

75 g/2³/₄ oz unsmoked bacon
or ham, diced

2 chicken livers, chopped

2 tbsp tomato purée

125 ml/4 fl oz dry white wine

salt and pepper

¹/₂ tsp freshly grated nutmeg

300 ml/10 fl oz chicken stock

125 ml/4 fl oz double cream

450 g/1 lb dried spaghetti

2 tbsp chopped fresh flat-leaf
parsley, to garnish

freshly grated Parmesan
cheese, to serve

## method

**1** Heat the olive oil and butter in a large saucepan over medium heat. Add the onion, carrot, celery and mushrooms to the pan, then cook until soft. Add the beef and bacon and cook until the beef is evenly browned.

**2** Stir in the chicken livers and tomato purée and cook for 2–3 minutes. Pour in the wine and season with salt, pepper and the nutmeg. Add the stock. Bring to the boil, then cover and simmer gently over low heat for 1 hour. Stir in the cream and simmer, uncovered, until reduced.

**3** Bring a large saucepan of lightly salted water to the boil. Add the pasta, return to the boil and cook until tender but still firm to the bite. Drain and transfer to a warmed serving dish.

**4** Spoon the sauce over the pasta, garnish with parsley and serve with Parmesan cheese.

# tagliatelle with a rich meat sauce

## ingredients

**SERVES 4**

4 tbsp olive oil, plus extra
　for serving
85 g/3 oz pancetta or rindless
　lean bacon, diced
1 onion, chopped
1 garlic clove, chopped finely
1 carrot, chopped
1 celery stalk, chopped
225 g/8 oz minced steak
115 g/4 oz chicken livers,
　chopped
2 tbsp strained tomatoes
125 ml/4 fl oz dry white wine
250 ml/8 fl oz beef stock or
　water
1 tbsp chopped fresh oregano
1 bay leaf
salt and pepper
450 g/1 lb dried tagliatelle
freshly grated Parmesan
　cheese, to serve

## method

**1** Heat the olive oil in a large, heavy-bottom saucepan. Add the pancetta or bacon and cook over medium heat, stirring occasionally, for 3–5 minutes, until it is just turning brown. Add the onion, garlic, carrot and celery and cook, stirring occasionally, for a further 5 minutes.

**2** Add the steak and cook over high heat, breaking up the meat with a wooden spoon, for 5 minutes, until browned. Stir in the chicken livers and cook, stirring occasionally, for a further 2–3 minutes. Add the strained tomatoes, wine, stock, oregano and bay leaf and season with salt and pepper. Bring to the boil, reduce the heat, cover and simmer for 30–35 minutes.

**3** When the sauce is almost cooked, bring a large saucepan of lightly salted water to the boil. Add the pasta, bring back to the boil and cook for 8–10 minutes, until tender but still firm to the bite. Drain, transfer to a warmed serving dish, drizzle with a little olive oil and toss well.

**4** Remove and discard the bay leaf from the sauce, then pour the sauce over the pasta, toss again and serve immediately with grated Parmesan cheese.

# pasta & pork in red wine sauce

## ingredients

**SERVES 4**

450 g/1 lb pork fillet,
    thinly sliced
4 tbsp olive oil
225 g/8 oz white mushrooms,
    sliced
1 tbsp lemon juice
pinch of saffron threads
350 g/12 oz dried orecchioni
4 tbsp double cream
12 quail eggs

### red wine sauce

1 tbsp olive oil
1 onion, chopped
1 tbsp tomato purée
200 ml/7 fl oz red wine
1 tsp oregano, finely chopped

## method

**1** To make the red wine sauce, heat the oil in a small, heavy-based saucepan, add the chopped onion and cook until transparent. Stir in the tomato purée, red wine and oregano. Heat gently to reduce and set aside.

**2** Pound the slices of pork between 2 sheets of clingfilm until wafer thin, then cut into strips. Heat the oil in a frying pan, add the pork and stir-fry for 5 minutes. Add the mushrooms to the pan and stir-fry for a further 2 minutes. Strain and pour over the red wine sauce. Reduce the heat and simmer for 20 minutes.

**3** Meanwhile, bring a large heavy-based saucepan of lightly salted water to the boil. Add the lemon juice, saffron and orecchioni, return to the boil and cook for 8–10 minutes, or until tender but still firm to the bite. Drain the pasta thoroughly, return to the pan and keep warm.

**4** Stir the cream into the pan with the pork and heat for a few minutes.

**5** Boil the quail eggs for 3 minutes, cool them in cold water and remove the shells. Transfer the pasta to a large, warmed serving plate, top with the pork and the sauce and garnish with the eggs. Serve immediately.

# chilli pork with tagliatelle

## ingredients

### SERVES 4

450 g/1 lb dried tagliatelle

3 tbsp peanut oil

350 g/12 oz pork fillet,
    cut into thin strips

1 garlic clove, finely chopped

1 bunch of spring onions,
    sliced

1-inch/2.5-cm piece fresh
    root ginger, grated

2 fresh Thai chillies,
    deseeded and finely
    chopped

1 red pepper, deseeded
    and cut into thin sticks

1 yellow pepper, deseeded
    and cut into thin sticks

3 courgettes cut into thin
    sticks

2 tbsp finely chopped peanuts

1 tsp ground cinnamon

1 tbsp oyster sauce

55 g/2 oz creamed coconut,
    grated

salt and pepper

2 tbsp chopped fresh
    coriander, to garnish

## method

**1** Bring a large, heavy-based saucepan of lightly salted water to the boil. Add the pasta, return to the boil and cook for 8–10 minutes, or until tender but still firm to the bite.

**2** Meanwhile, heat the peanut oil in a preheated wok or large, heavy-based frying pan. Add the pork and stir-fry for 5 minutes. Add the garlic, spring onions, ginger and Thai chillies and stir-fry for 2 minutes.

**3** Add the red and yellow peppers and the courgettes and stir-fry for 1 minute. Add the peanuts, cinnamon, oyster sauce and creamed coconut and stir-fry for a further 1 minute. Season with salt and pepper. Drain the pasta and transfer to a serving dish. Top with the chilli pork, sprinkle with the chopped coriander and serve.

# spaghetti alla carbonara

## ingredients

**SERVES 4**

450 g/1 lb dried spaghetti

1 tbsp olive oil

225 g/8 oz rindless pancetta
    or lean bacon, chopped

4 eggs

5 tbsp single cream

salt and pepper

4 tbsp freshly grated
    Parmesan cheese

## method

**1** Bring a large, heavy-based saucepan of lightly salted water to the boil. Add the pasta, return to the boil and cook for 8–10 minutes, or until tender but still firm to the bite.

**2** Meanwhile, heat the olive oil in a heavy-based frying pan. Add the chopped pancetta and cook over medium heat, stirring frequently, for 8–10 minutes.

**3** Beat the eggs with the cream in a small bowl and season with salt and pepper. Drain the pasta and return it to the saucepan. Tip in the contents of the frying pan, then add the egg mixture and half the Parmesan cheese. Stir well, then transfer to a warmed serving dish. Serve immediately, sprinkled with the remaining Parmesan cheese.

# rigatoni with spicy bacon & tomato sauce

## ingredients

**SERVES 4**

6 tbsp olive oil

3 garlic cloves, sliced thinly

75 g/2³/4 oz bacon, chopped

800 g/1 lb 12 oz canned
    chopped tomatoes

¹/2 tsp dried chilli flakes

salt and pepper

450 g/1 lb rigatoni

10 fresh basil leaves, shredded

2 tbsp freshly grated romano
    cheese

## method

**1** Heat the oil and garlic in a large frying pan over medium–low heat. Cook until the garlic is just beginning to colour. Add the bacon and cook until browned.

**2** Stir in the tomatoes and chilli flakes. Season with a little salt and pepper. Bring to the boil, then simmer over medium–low heat for 30–40 minutes, until the oil separates from the tomatoes.

**3** Cook the pasta in plenty of boiling salted water until tender but still firm to the bite. Drain and transfer to a warmed serving dish.

**4** Pour the sauce over the pasta. Add the shredded basil and grated romano, then toss well to mix. Serve at once.

# linguine with bacon & olives

## ingredients

**SERVES 4**

3 tbsp olive oil

2 onions, thinly sliced

2 garlic cloves, finely chopped

175 g/6 oz rindless lean
    bacon, diced

225 g/8 oz mushrooms, sliced

5 canned anchovy fillets,
    drained

6 black olives, pitted
    and halved

salt and pepper

450 g/1 lb dried linguine

25 g/1 oz freshly grated
    Parmesan cheese

## method

**1** Heat the olive oil in a large frying pan.
Add the onions, garlic and bacon and cook
over low heat, stirring occasionally, until the
onions are softened. Stir in the mushrooms,
anchovies and olives, then season with salt, if
necessary, and pepper. Simmer for 5 minutes.

**2** Meanwhile, bring a large heavy-based
saucepan of lightly salted water to the boil.
Add the pasta, return to the boil and cook for
8–10 minutes, or until tender but still firm to
the bite.

**3** Drain the pasta and transfer to a warmed
serving dish. Spoon the sauce on top, toss
lightly and sprinkle with the Parmesan cheese.
Serve immediately.

# saffron linguine

## ingredients

### SERVES 4

350 g/12 oz dried linguine

pinch of saffron threads

2 tbsp water

140 g/5 oz ham, cut into strips

175 ml/6 fl oz double cream

55 g/2 oz freshly grated
    Parmesan cheese

salt and pepper

2 egg yolks

## method

**1** Bring a large, heavy-based saucepan of lightly salted water to the boil. Add the pasta, return to the boil and cook for 8–10 minutes, or until tender but still firm to the bite.

**2** Meanwhile, place the saffron in a separate heavy-based saucepan and add the water. Bring to the boil, then remove from the heat and let stand for 5 minutes.

**3** Stir the ham, cream and grated Parmesan cheese into the saffron and return the pan to the heat. Season with salt and pepper and heat through gently, stirring constantly, until simmering. Remove the pan from the heat and beat in the egg yolks. Drain the pasta and transfer to a large, warmed serving dish. Add the saffron sauce, toss well and serve.

# rigatoni with ham, tomato & chilli sauce

## ingredients

**SERVES 4**

1 tbsp olive oil

2 tbsp butter

1 onion, chopped finely

150 g/5$^1$/$_2$ oz ham, diced

2 garlic cloves, chopped
   very finely

1 fresh red chilli, deseeded
   and chopped finely

800 g/1 lb 12 oz canned
   chopped tomatoes

salt and pepper

450 g/1 lb rigatoni or penne

2 tbsp chopped fresh flat-leaf
   parsley

6 tbsp freshly grated Parmesan
   cheese

## method

**1** Put the olive oil and 1 tablespoon of the butter in a large saucepan over medium–low heat. Add the onion and fry for 10 minutes until soft and golden. Add the ham and fry for 5 minutes until lightly browned. Stir in the garlic, chilli and tomatoes. Season with a little salt and pepper. Bring to the boil, then simmer over medium-low heat for 30–40 minutes until thickened.

**2** Cook the pasta in plenty of boiling salted water until tender but still firm to the bite. Drain and transfer to a warmed serving dish.

**3** Pour the sauce over the pasta. Add the parsley, Parmesan cheese and the remaining butter. Toss well to mix and serve immediately.

# macaroni with sausage, pepperoncini & olives

## ingredients

**SERVES 4**

1 tbsp olive oil

1 large onion, chopped finely

2 garlic cloves, minced

450 g/1 lb pork sausage, peeled and chopped coarsely

3 canned pepperoncini, or other hot red peppers, drained and sliced

400 g/14 oz canned chopped tomatoes

2 tsp dried oregano

125 ml/4 fl oz chicken stock or red wine

salt and pepper

450 g/1 lb dried macaroni

12–15 black olives, pitted and cut into quarters

75 g/2¾ oz freshly grated cheese, such as Cheddar or Gruyère

## method

**1** Heat the oil in a large frying pan over medium heat. Add the onion and fry for 5 minutes until soft. Add the garlic and fry for a few seconds until just beginning to colour. Add the sausage and fry until evenly browned.

**2** Stir in the pepperoncini, tomatoes, oregano and stock. Season with salt and pepper. Bring to the boil, then simmer over medium heat for 10 minutes, stirring occasionally.

**3** Cook the macaroni in plenty of boiling salted water until tender but still firm to the bite. Drain and transfer to a warmed serving dish.

**4** Add the olives and half the cheese to the sauce, then stir until the cheese has melted. Pour the sauce over the pasta. Toss well to mix. Sprinkle with the remaining cheese and serve at once.

# pepperoni pasta

## ingredients

**SERVES 4**

3 tbsp olive oil

1 onion, chopped

1 red pepper, deseeded
and diced

1 orange pepper, deseeded
and diced

800 g/1 lb 12 oz canned
chopped tomatoes

1 tbsp sun-dried tomato
purée

1 tsp paprika

225 g/8 oz pepperoni, sliced

2 tbsp chopped fresh flat-leaf
parsley, plus extra to garnish

salt and pepper

450 g/1 lb dried garganelli

mixed salad leaves and vine
tomatoes, to serve

## method

**1** Heat 2 tablespoons of the olive oil in a large,
heavy-based frying pan. Add the onion and
cook over low heat, stirring occasionally, for
5 minutes, or until softened. Add the red and
orange peppers, tomatoes and their can
juices, sun-dried tomato purée and paprika to
the pan and bring to the boil.

**2** Add the pepperoni and parsley and season
with salt and pepper. Stir well and bring to the
boil, then reduce the heat and simmer for
10–15 minutes.

**3** Meanwhile, bring a large, heavy-based
saucepan of lightly salted water to the boil.
Add the pasta, return to the boil and cook for
8–10 minutes, or until tender but still firm to
the bite. Drain well and transfer to a warmed
serving dish. Add the remaining olive oil and
toss. Add the sauce and toss again. Sprinkle
with parsley and serve immediately with mixed
salad leaves and vine tomatoes.

# chorizo & mushroom pasta

## ingredients

**SERVES 6**

680 g/1 lb 8 oz dried vermicelli

125 ml/4 fl oz olive oil

2 garlic cloves

125 g/4$^1$/$_2$ oz chorizo, sliced

225 g/8 oz exotic mushrooms

3 fresh red chillies, chopped

salt and pepper

2 tbsp fresh Parmesan cheese
    shavings, for sprinkling

10 anchovy fillets, to garnish

## method

**1** Bring a large, heavy-based saucepan of lightly salted water to the boil. Add the vermicelli, return to the boil and cook for 8–10 minutes, or until just tender, but still firm to the bite. Drain the pasta thoroughly, then place on a large, warmed serving plate and keep warm.

**2** Meanwhile, heat the olive oil in a frying pan. Add the garlic and cook for 1 minute. Add the chorizo and exotic mushrooms and cook for 4 minutes. Add the chopped chillies and cook for a further minute.

**3** Pour the chorizo and exotic mushroom mixture over the vermicelli and season with salt and pepper. Sprinkle with fresh Parmesan cheese shavings, garnish with anchovy fillets and serve at once.

# linguine with lamb & yellow pepper sauce

## ingredients

### SERVES 4

4 tbsp olive oil

280 g/10 oz boneless lamb, cubed

1 garlic clove, finely chopped

1 bay leaf

125 ml/4 fl oz dry white wine

salt and pepper

2 large yellow peppers, deseeded and diced

4 tomatoes, peeled and chopped

250 g/9 oz dried linguine

## method

1 Heat half the olive oil in a large, heavy-based frying pan. Add the lamb and cook over medium heat, stirring frequently, until browned on all sides. Add the garlic and cook for a further minute. Add the bay leaf, pour in the wine and season with salt and pepper. Bring to the boil and cook for 5 minutes, or until reduced.

2 Stir in the remaining oil, peppers and tomatoes. Reduce the heat, cover and simmer, stirring occasionally, for 45 minutes.

3 Meanwhile, bring a large, heavy-based saucepan of lightly salted water to the boil. Add the pasta, return to the boil and cook for 8–10 minutes, or until tender but still firm to the bite. Drain and transfer to a warmed serving dish. Remove and discard the bay leaf from the lamb sauce and spoon the sauce onto the pasta. Toss well and serve at once.

# chicken with basil & pine nut pesto

## ingredients

**SERVES 4**

2 tbsp vegetable oil

4 skinless, boneless
    chicken breasts

350 g/12 oz dried farfalle

salt and pepper

sprig of fresh basil, to garnish

### pesto

100 g/3$^1$/$_2$ oz shredded
    fresh basil

125 ml/4 fl oz extra-virgin
    olive oil

3 tbsp pine nuts

3 garlic cloves, minced

55 g/2 oz freshly grated
    Parmesan cheese

2 tbsp freshly grated romano
    cheese

## method

**1** To make the pesto, place the basil, olive oil, pine nuts, garlic and a generous pinch of salt in a food processor or blender and process until smooth. Scrape the mixture into a bowl and stir in the cheeses.

**2** Heat the vegetable oil in a frying pan over medium heat. Fry the chicken breasts, turning once, for 8–10 minutes, or until the juices are no longer pink. Cut into small cubes.

**3** Cook the pasta in plenty of lightly salted boiling water until tender but still firm to the bite. Drain and transfer to a warmed serving dish. Add the chicken and pesto, then season with pepper. Toss well to mix.

**4** Garnish with a basil sprig and serve warm.

# tagliatelle with creamy chicken & shiitake sauce

## ingredients

**SERVES 4**

25 g/1 oz dried shiitake
    mushrooms

350 ml/12 fl oz hot water

1 tbsp olive oil

6 bacon slices, chopped

3 boneless, skinless chicken
    breasts, sliced into strips

115 g/4 oz fresh shiitake
    mushrooms, sliced

1 small onion, chopped finely

1 tsp fresh oregano or
    marjoram, chopped finely

275 ml/9 fl oz chicken stock

300 ml/10 fl oz double cream

salt and pepper

450 g/1 lb dried tagliatelle

55 g/2 oz freshly grated
    Parmesan cheese

chopped fresh flat-leaf
    parsley, to garnish

## method

**1** Put the dried mushrooms in a bowl with the hot water and soak for 30 minutes, or until softened. Remove, squeezing excess water back into the bowl. Strain the liquid in a fine-meshed sieve and reserve. Slice the soaked mushrooms, discarding the stems.

**2** Heat the oil in a large frying pan over medium heat. Add the bacon and chicken, then stir-fry for about 3 minutes. Add the dried and fresh mushrooms, onion and oregano. Stir-fry for 5–7 minutes, or until soft. Pour in the stock and the mushroom liquid. Bring to the boil, stirring. Simmer for about 10 minutes, continuing to stir, until reduced. Add the cream and simmer for 5 minutes, stirring, until beginning to thicken. Season with salt and pepper. Remove the pan from the heat and set aside.

**3** Cook the pasta until tender but still firm to the bite. Drain and transfer to a serving dish. Pour the sauce over the pasta. Add half the Parmesan cheese and mix. Sprinkle with parsley and serve with the remaining Parmesan cheese.

# pappardelle with chicken & porcini

## ingredients

**SERVES 4**

40 g/1¹/₂ oz dried porcini
    mushrooms
175 ml/6 fl oz hot water
800 g/1 lb 12 oz canned
    chopped tomatoes
1 fresh red chilli, deseeded
    and finely chopped
3 tbsp olive oil
350 g/12 oz skinless, boneless
    chicken, cut into thin strips
2 garlic cloves, finely chopped
350 g/12 oz dried pappardelle
salt and pepper
2 tbsp chopped fresh flat-leaf
    parsley, to garnish

## method

**1** Place the porcini in a small bowl, add the hot water and soak for 30 minutes. Meanwhile, place the tomatoes and their can juices in a heavy-based saucepan and break them up with a wooden spoon, then stir in the chilli. Bring to the boil, then reduce the heat and simmer, stirring occasionally, for 30 minutes, or until reduced.

**2** Remove the mushrooms from their soaking liquid with a slotted spoon, reserving the liquid. Strain the liquid into the tomatoes through a sieve lined with cheesecloth and simmer for a further 15 minutes. Meanwhile, heat 2 tablespoons of the olive oil in a heavy-based frying pan. Add the chicken and cook, stirring frequently, until golden brown all over and tender. Stir in the mushrooms and garlic and cook for a further 5 minutes.

**3** Bring a large, heavy-based saucepan of lightly salted water to the boil. Add the pasta, return to the boil and cook for 8–10 minutes, or until tender but still firm to the bite. Drain well, then transfer to a warmed serving dish. Drizzle the pasta with the remaining olive oil and toss lightly. Stir the chicken mixture into the tomato sauce, season with salt and pepper and spoon onto the pasta. Toss lightly, sprinkle with parsley and serve at once.

# farfalle with chicken, broccoli & roasted red peppers

## ingredients

**SERVES 4**

4 tbsp olive oil

5 tbsp butter

3 garlic cloves, chopped very finely

450 g/1 lb boneless, skinless chicken breasts, diced

$1/4$ tsp dried chilli flakes

salt and pepper

450 g/1 lb small broccoli florets

300 g/10$1/2$ oz dried farfalle or fusilli

175 g/6 oz bottled roasted red peppers, drained and diced

250 ml/9 fl oz chicken stock

freshly grated Parmesan cheese, to serve (optional)

## method

**1** Bring a large saucepan of salted water to the boil. Meanwhile, place the olive oil, butter and garlic in a large frying pan over medium–low heat. Cook the garlic until just beginning to colour.

**2** Add the diced chicken, then raise the heat to medium and stir-fry for 4–5 minutes, or until the chicken is no longer pink. Add the chilli flakes and season with salt and pepper. Remove from the heat.

**3** Plunge the broccoli into the boiling water and cook for 2 minutes, or until tender-crisp. Remove with a perforated spoon and set aside. Bring the water back to the boil. Add the pasta and cook until tender but still firm to the bite. Drain and add to the chicken mixture in the pan. Add the broccoli and roasted peppers, then pour in the stock. Simmer briskly over medium-high heat, stirring frequently, until most of the liquid has been absorbed.

**4** Serve sprinkled with the Parmesan cheese, if using.

# spaghetti with parsley chicken

## ingredients

**SERVES 4**

1 tbsp olive oil

thinly pared rind of 1 lemon,
    cut into julienne strips

1 tsp finely chopped fresh
    root ginger

1 tsp sugar

salt

250 ml/8 fl oz chicken stock

250 g/9 oz dried spaghetti

4 tbsp butter

225 g/8 oz skinless, boneless
    chicken breasts, diced

1 red onion, finely chopped

leaves from 2 bunches of
    flat-leaf parsley

## method

**1** Heat the olive oil in a heavy-based saucepan. Add most of the lemon rind, reserving a few strips to garnish, and cook over low heat, stirring frequently, for 5 minutes. Stir in the ginger and sugar, season with salt and cook, stirring constantly, for a further 2 minutes. Pour in the chicken stock, bring to the boil, then cook for 5 minutes, or until the liquid has reduced by half.

**2** Meanwhile, bring a large, heavy-based saucepan of lightly salted water to the boil. Add the pasta, return to the boil and cook for 8–10 minutes, or until tender but still firm to the bite.

**3** Meanwhile, melt half the butter in a frying pan. Add the chicken and onion and cook, stirring frequently, for 5 minutes, or until the chicken is light brown all over. Stir in the lemon and ginger mixture and cook for 1 minute. Stir in the parsley leaves and cook, stirring constantly, for a further 3 minutes.

**4** Drain the pasta and transfer to a warmed serving dish, then add the remaining butter and toss well. Add the chicken sauce, toss again and serve, garnished with the reserved lemon rind strips.

# fettuccine with chicken & onion cream sauce

## ingredients

**SERVES 4**

1 tbsp olive oil

2 tbsp butter

1 garlic clove, chopped
    very finely

4 boneless, skinless chicken
    breasts

salt and pepper

1 onion, chopped finely

1 chicken bouillon cube,
    crumbled

125 ml/4 fl oz water·

300 ml/10 fl oz double cream

175 ml/6 fl oz milk

6 spring onions, green part
    included, sliced diagonally

35 g/1¼ oz freshly grated
    Parmesan cheese

450 g/1 lb dried fettuccine

chopped fresh flat-leaf
    parsley, to garnish

## method

**1** Heat the oil and butter with the garlic in a large frying pan over medium–low heat. Cook the garlic until just beginning to colour. Add the chicken breasts and raise the heat to medium. Cook for 4–5 minutes on each side, or until the juices are no longer pink. Season with salt and pepper. Remove from the heat. Remove the chicken breasts, leaving the oil in the pan. Slice the breasts diagonally into thin strips and set aside.

**2** Reheat the oil in the frying pan. Add the onion and cook gently for 5 minutes, or until soft. Add the crumbled bouillon cube and the water. Bring to the boil, then simmer over medium–low heat for 10 minutes. Stir in the cream, milk, spring onions and Parmesan cheese. Simmer until heated through and slightly thickened.

**3** Cook the fettuccine in boiling salted water until tender but still firm to the bite. Drain and transfer to a warmed serving dish. Layer the chicken slices over the pasta. Pour on the sauce, then garnish with parsley and serve.

# creamy chicken ravioli

## ingredients

**SERVES 4**

115 g/4 oz cooked skinless,
   boneless chicken breast,
   coarsely chopped

55 g/2 oz cooked spinach

55 g/2 oz prosciutto, coarsely
   chopped

1 shallot, coarsely chopped

6 tbsp freshly grated romano
   cheese

pinch of freshly grated nutmeg

2 eggs, lightly beaten

salt and pepper

1 quantity basic pasta dough
   (see below)

plain flour, for dusting

300 ml/10 fl oz double cream

2 garlic cloves,
   finely chopped

115 g/4 oz chestnut
   mushrooms, thinly sliced

2 tbsp shredded fresh basil

fresh basil sprigs, to garnish

### pasta dough

200 g/7 oz plain flour, plus
   extra for dusting

pinch of salt

2 eggs, lightly beaten

1 tbsp olive oil

## method

**1** To make the pasta dough, sift the flour into a food processor. Add the salt, eggs and olive oil and process until the dough begins to come together. Knead on a lightly floured board until smooth. Cover and let rest for 30 minutes.

**2** Process the chicken, spinach, prosciutto and shallot in a food processor until chopped and blended. Transfer to a bowl, stir in 2 tablespoons of the romano cheese, the nutmeg and half the egg, and season.

**3** Halve the pasta dough and thinly roll out each half on a lightly floured board. Place small mounds of the filling in rows 4 cm/1¹/₂ inches apart on one sheet of dough and brush in between with beaten egg. Cover with the other half of dough. Press down between the mounds of filling, pushing out any air. Cut into squares and let rest on a floured tea towel for 1 hour.

**4** Bring a saucepan of salted water to the boil. Add the ravioli, in batches, return to the boil and cook for 5 minutes. Remove and drain on kitchen paper, then transfer to a warmed dish.

**5** Meanwhile, bring the cream to the boil with the garlic in a frying pan. Simmer for 1 minute, then add the mushrooms and 2 tablespoons of the remaining cheese. Season, simmer for 3 minutes, then stir in the basil. Pour the sauce over the ravioli, sprinkle with the remaining cheese, garnish with basil sprigs and serve.

# chicken tortellini

## ingredients

**SERVES 4**

115 g/4 oz skinless, boneless
    chicken breast

55 g/2 oz prosciutto

40 g/1$^1$/$_2$ oz cooked spinach,
    well drained

1 tbsp finely
    chopped onion

2 tbsp freshly grated
    Parmesan cheese

pinch of ground allspice

1 egg, beaten

salt and pepper

double quantity pasta dough
    (see page 86)

2 tbsp chopped fresh
    flat-leaf parsley, to garnish

### sauce

300 ml/10 fl oz single cream

2 garlic cloves, crushed

115 g/4 oz white mushrooms,
    thinly sliced

salt and pepper

4 tbsp freshly grated
    Parmesan cheese

## method

**1** Bring a saucepan of lightly salted water
to the boil. Add the chicken and poach for
10 minutes. Cool slightly, then place in a food
processor with the prosciutto, spinach and
onion and process until finely chopped. Stir in
the Parmesan cheese, allspice and egg and
season with salt and pepper.

**2** Thinly roll out the pasta dough and cut into
4–5-cm/1$^1$/$_2$–2-inch circles. Place $^1$/$_2$ teaspoon
of the chicken and ham filling in the centre of
each circle. Fold the pieces in half and press
the edges to seal, then wrap each piece
around your index finger, cross over the ends
and curl the rest of the dough backward to
make a navel shape. Re-roll the trimmings
and repeat until all the dough is used up.

**3** Bring a saucepan of salted water to the boil.
Add the tortellini, in batches, return to the boil
and cook for 5 minutes. Drain the tortellini
well and transfer to a serving dish.

**4** To make the sauce, bring the cream and
garlic to the boil in a small saucepan, then
simmer for 3 minutes. Add the mushrooms
and half the cheese, season with salt and
pepper and simmer for 2–3 minutes. Pour
the sauce over the tortellini. Sprinkle over the
remaining Parmesan cheese, garnish with the
parsley and serve.

# seafood

Pasta combined with seafood gives a light, elegant, delicate result that is ideal for midweek suppers and for lunch parties. Even when the recipe calls for a fairly robust pasta, such as Mafalde with Fresh Salmon, Fusilli with Monkfish & Broccoli or Springtime Pasta, you will finish your meal feeling comfortably satisfied and your digestive system will not be overwhelmed.

A great store-cupboard standby is Pasta with Tuna, Garlic, Lemon, Capers & Olives – if you keep a pot of fresh parsley growing on your windowsill, you can be ready to make this quick dish any time. When a stylish recipe is the order of the day, dishes such as Fettuccine with Sole & Monkfish, Linguine with Smoked Salmon & Rocket, Crab Ravioli and Fettuccine with Scallops in Porcini & Cream Sauce are perfect – they almost look too good to eat. If you are passionate about shellfish, try Mixed Shellfish with Angel-hair Pasta, Spaghetti with Clams, Tagliatelle & Mussels with White Wine, Garlic & Parsley or Seafood Pasta Pockets – you can serve these in the baking parchment packages they are cooked in.

Fusion food is now very popular and an excellent example of how well this can work is Fusilli with Hot Cajun Seafood Sauce – it's completely cross-cultural and tastes absolutely divine!

# fettuccine with sole & monkfish

## ingredients

**SERVES 4**

85 g/3 oz plain flour

salt and pepper

450 g/1 lb lemon sole fillets,
   skinned and cut into chunks

450 g/1 lb monkfish fillets,
   skinned and cut into chunks

85 g/3 oz unsalted butter

4 shallots, finely chopped

2 garlic cloves, crushed

1 carrot, diced

1 leek, finely chopped

300 ml/10 fl oz fish stock

300 ml/10 fl oz
   dry white wine

2 tsp anchovy essence

1 tbsp balsamic vinegar

450 g/1 lb dried fettuccine

chopped fresh flat-leaf
   parsley, to garnish

## method

**1** Season the flour with salt and pepper and spread out 2 tablespoons on a plate. Coat all the fish pieces with it, shaking off the excess. Melt the butter in a heavy-based saucepan or flameproof casserole. Add the fish, shallots, garlic, carrot and leek, then cook over low heat, stirring frequently, for 10 minutes. Sprinkle in the remaining seasoned flour and cook, stirring constantly, for 1 minute.

**2** Mix the fish stock, wine, anchovy essence and balsamic vinegar together in a jug and gradually stir into the fish mixture. Bring to the boil, stirring constantly, then reduce the heat and simmer gently for 35 minutes.

**3** Meanwhile, bring a large heavy-based saucepan of lightly salted water to the boil. Add the pasta, return to the boil and cook for 8–10 minutes, or until tender but still firm to the bite. Drain and transfer to a warmed serving dish. Spoon the fish mixture onto the pasta, garnish with chopped parsley and serve immediately.

# linguine with smoked salmon & rocket

## ingredients

**SERVES 4**

350 g/12 oz dried linguine

2 tbsp olive oil

1 garlic clove, finely chopped

115 g/4 oz smoked salmon,
    cut into thin strips

55 g/2 oz rocket

salt and pepper

4 lemon halves, to garnish

## method

**1** Bring a large, heavy-based saucepan of lightly salted water to the boil. Add the pasta, return to the boil and cook for 8–10 minutes, or until tender but still firm to the bite.

**2** Just before the end of the cooking time, heat the olive oil in a heavy-based frying pan. Add the garlic and cook over low heat, stirring constantly, for 1 minute. Do not allow the garlic to brown or it will taste bitter. Add the salmon and rocket. Season with salt and pepper and cook, stirring constantly, for 1 minute. Remove the pan from the heat.

**3** Drain the pasta and transfer to a warmed dish. Add the smoked salmon and rocket mixture, toss lightly and serve, garnished with lemon halves.

# conchiglie with smoked salmon, sour cream & mustard sauce

## ingredients

**SERVES 4**

450 g/1 lb conchiglie or
    tagliatelle

300 ml/10 fl oz sour cream

2 tsp Dijon mustard

4 large spring onions, sliced
    finely

225 g/8 oz smoked salmon,
    cut into bite-sized pieces

finely grated rind of $1/2$ lemon

pepper

2 tbsp chopped fresh chives
    plus whole chives, to
    garnish

## method

**1** Cook the pasta in plenty of boiling salted water until tender but still firm to the bite. Drain and return to the saucepan. Add the sour cream, mustard, spring onions, smoked salmon and lemon rind to the pasta. Stir over low heat until heated through. Season to taste with pepper.

**2** Transfer to a serving dish. Sprinkle with the chopped chives. Serve warm or at room temperature, garnished with whole chives.

# mafalde with fresh salmon

## ingredients

**SERVES 4**

350 g/12 oz salmon fillet

fresh dill sprigs, plus extra
    to garnish

125 ml/8 fl oz dry white wine

salt and pepper

6 tomatoes, peeled
    and chopped

150 ml/5 fl oz double cream

350 g/12 oz dried mafalde,
    tagliatelle or fettuccine

115 g/4 oz cooked, shelled
    prawns

## method

**1** Place the salmon in a large, heavy-based frying pan. Add a few dill sprigs, pour in the wine and season with salt and pepper. Bring to the boil, then reduce the heat, cover and poach gently for 5 minutes, or until the flesh flakes easily. Remove with a spatula, reserving the cooking liquid, and cool slightly. Remove and discard the skin and any remaining small bones, then flake the flesh into large chunks.

**2** Add the tomatoes and cream to the reserved liquid. Bring to the boil, then reduce the heat and simmer for 15 minutes, or until the sauce has thickened.

**3** Meanwhile, bring a large, heavy-based saucepan of lightly salted water to the boil. Add the pasta, return to the boil and cook for 8–10 minutes, or until tender but still firm to the bite. Drain and transfer to a warmed serving dish.

**4** Add the salmon and prawns to the tomato sauce and stir gently until coated. Spoon the sauce onto the pasta, toss lightly, then serve, garnished with dill sprigs.

# italian fish stew with ziti

## ingredients

### SERVES 4

pinch of saffron threads

1 litre/32 fl oz fish stock

4 tbsp butter

450 g/1 lb red snapper fillets,
thinly sliced

12 prepared scallops

12 raw jumbo prawns, shelled
and deveined

225 g/8 oz raw prawns,
shelled and deveined

salt and pepper

finely grated rind and juice
of 1 lemon

150 ml/5 fl oz white wine
vinegar

150 ml/5 fl oz white wine

150 ml/5 fl oz double cream

3 tbsp chopped fresh flat-leaf
parsley

450 g/1 lb dried ziti

## method

**1** Place the saffron in a small bowl, add
3 tablespoons of the fish stock and let soak.
Melt the butter in a large heavy-based
saucepan or flameproof casserole. Add the
red snapper, scallops and both types of
prawns and cook over medium heat, stirring
frequently, for 3–5 minutes, or until the prawns
have changed colour. Season with pepper and
add the grated rind and lemon juice. Transfer
the fish and shellfish to a plate and keep warm.

**2** Pour the remaining stock into the pan and
add the saffron and its soaking liquid. Bring to
the boil and cook until reduced by about one
third. Add the vinegar and continue to boil for
4 minutes. Stir in the white wine and cook
for 5 minutes, or until reduced and thickened.
Add the cream and parsley, then season
with salt and pepper and simmer gently for
2 minutes.

**3** Meanwhile, bring a large, heavy-based
saucepan of lightly salted water to the boil.
Add the pasta, return to the boil and cook for
8–10 minutes, or until tender but still firm to
the bite. Drain well and transfer to a large,
warmed serving platter. Arrange the fish and
shellfish on top and pour over the sauce.
Serve immediately.

# fusilli with monkfish & broccoli

## ingredients

**SERVES 4**

115 g/4 oz head of broccoli, divided into florets

3 tbsp olive oil

350 g/12 oz monkfish fillet, skinned and cut into bite-size pieces

2 garlic cloves, crushed

salt and pepper

125 ml/4 fl oz dry white wine

225 ml/8 fl oz double cream

400 g/14 oz dried fusilli bucati

85 g/3 oz Gorgonzola cheese, diced

## method

**1** Divide the broccoli florets into tiny sprigs. Bring a saucepan of lightly salted water to the boil, add the broccoli and cook for 2 minutes. Drain and refresh under cold running water.

**2** Heat the olive oil in a large, heavy-based frying pan. Add the monkfish and garlic and season with salt and pepper. Cook, stirring frequently, for 5 minutes, or until the fish is opaque. Pour in the white wine and cream and cook, stirring occasionally, for 5 minutes, or until the fish is cooked through and the sauce has thickened. Stir in the broccoli sprigs.

**3** Meanwhile, bring a large, heavy-based saucepan of lightly salted water to the boil. Add the pasta, return to the boil and cook for 8–10 minutes, or until tender but still firm to the bite. Drain the pasta and tip it into the pan with the fish, add the cheese and toss lightly. Serve immediately.

# penne with squid & tomatoes

## ingredients

**SERVES 4**

225 g/8 oz dried penne

350 g/12 oz prepared squid

6 tbsp olive oil

2 onions, sliced

250 ml/8 fl oz fish or
    chicken stock

150 ml/5 fl oz full-bodied
    red wine

400 g/14 oz canned chopped
    tomatoes

2 tbsp tomato purée

1 tbsp chopped fresh marjoram

1 bay leaf

salt and pepper

2 tbsp chopped fresh parsley

## method

**1** Bring a large, heavy-based saucepan of lightly salted water to the boil. Add the pasta, return to the boil and cook for 3 minutes, then drain and set aside until required. With a sharp knife, cut the squid into strips.

**2** Heat the olive oil in a large flameproof dish or casserole. Add the onions and cook over low heat, stirring occasionally, for 5 minutes, or until softened. Add the squid and fish stock, bring to the boil and simmer for 3 minutes. Stir in the wine, chopped tomatoes and their can juices, tomato purée, marjoram and bay leaf. Season with salt and pepper. Bring to the boil and cook for 5 minutes, or until slightly reduced.

**3** Add the pasta, return to the boil and simmer for 5–7 minutes, or until tender but still firm to the bite. Remove and discard the bay leaf, stir in the parsley and serve at once.

# pasta with tuna, garlic, lemon, capers & olives

## ingredients

SERVES 4

350 g/12 oz dried conchiglie
   or gnocchi

4 tbsp olive oil

4 tbsp butter

3 large garlic cloves,
   sliced thinly

200 g/7 oz canned tuna,
   drained and broken
   into chunks

2 tbsp lemon juice

1 tbsp capers, drained

10–12 black olives, pitted
   and sliced

2 tbsp chopped fresh
   flat-leaf parsley

mixed salad leaves, to serve

## method

**1** Cook the pasta or gnocchi in plenty of boiling salted water until tender but still firm to the bite. Drain and return to the saucepan.

**2** Heat the olive oil and half the butter in a frying pan over medium–low heat. Add the garlic and cook for a few seconds until just beginning to colour. Reduce the heat to low. Add the tuna, lemon juice, capers and olives. Stir gently until all the ingredients are heated through.

**3** Transfer the pasta or gnocchi to a warmed serving dish. Pour the tuna mixture over the pasta. Add the parsley and remaining butter. Toss well to mix, then serve immediately with mixed salad leaves.

# spaghetti with tuna & parsley

## ingredients

**SERVES 4**

500 g/1 lb 2 oz dried
    spaghetti

25 g/1 oz butter

fresh flat-leaf parsley sprigs,
    to garnish

black olives, to serve
    (optional)

sauce

200 g/7 oz canned tuna,
    drained

55 g/2 oz canned anchovies,
    drained

250 ml/9 fl oz olive oil

55 g/2 oz coarsely chopped
    fresh flat-leaf parsley

150 ml/5 fl oz soured cream
    or yogurt

salt and pepper

## method

**1** Bring a large, heavy-based saucepan of lightly salted water to the boil. Add the spaghetti, return to the boil and cook for 8–10 minutes, or until tender but still firm to the bite. Drain the spaghetti in a colander and return to the pan. Add the butter, toss thoroughly to coat and keep warm until required.

**2** Flake the tuna into smaller pieces using 2 forks. Place the tuna in a blender or food processor with the anchovies, olive oil and parsley and process until the sauce is smooth. Pour in the soured cream or yogurt and process for a few seconds to blend. Taste the sauce and season with salt and pepper, if necessary.

**3** Warm 4 plates. Shake the pan of spaghetti over medium heat for a few minutes, or until it is thoroughly warmed through.

**4** Pour the sauce over the spaghetti and toss quickly, using 2 forks. Serve immediately with a small dish of black olives, if liked.

# linguine alla puttanesca

## ingredients

### SERVES 4

450 g/1 lb plum tomatoes

3 tbsp olive oil

2 garlic cloves, finely chopped

10 anchovy fillets, drained
and chopped

140 g/5 oz black olives, pitted
and chopped

1 tbsp capers, rinsed

pinch of cayenne pepper

400 g/14 oz dried linguine

salt

2 tbsp chopped fresh flat-leaf
parsley, to garnish

crusty bread, to serve

## method

**1** Peel the tomatoes by cutting a cross in the bottom of each and placing in a heatproof bowl. Cover with boiling water and let stand for 35–45 seconds. Drain and plunge into cold water, then the skins will slide off easily. Deseed and chop the tomatoes.

**2** Heat the olive oil in a heavy-based saucepan. Add the garlic and cook over low heat, stirring frequently, for 2 minutes. Add the anchovies and mash them to a pulp with a fork. Add the olives, capers and tomatoes and season with cayenne pepper. Cover and simmer for 25 minutes.

**3** Meanwhile, bring a saucepan of lightly salted water to the boil. Add the pasta, return to the boil and cook for 8–10 minutes, or until tender but still firm to the bite. Drain and transfer to a warmed serving dish.

**4** Spoon the anchovy sauce into the dish and toss the pasta, using 2 large forks. Garnish with the parsley and serve immediately with crusty bread.

# spinach & anchovy pasta

## ingredients

### SERVES 4

900 g/2 lb fresh, young
    spinach leaves
400 g/14 oz dried fettuccine
5 tbsp olive oil
3 tbsp pine nuts
3 garlic cloves, crushed
8 canned anchovy fillets,
    drained and chopped

## method

**1** Trim off any tough spinach stalks. Rinse the spinach leaves under cold running water and place them in a large saucepan with only the water that is clinging to them after washing. Cover and cook over high heat, shaking the pan from time to time, until the spinach has wilted, but retains its colour. Drain well, set aside and keep warm.

**2** Bring a large heavy-based saucepan of lightly salted water to the boil. Add the fettuccine, return to the boil and cook for 8–10 minutes, or until it is just tender but still firm to the bite.

**3** Heat 4 tablespoons of the olive oil in a separate saucepan. Add the pine nuts and cook until golden. Remove the pine nuts from the pan and set aside.

**4** Add the garlic to the pan and cook until golden. Add the anchovies and stir in the spinach. Cook, stirring, for 2–3 minutes, until heated through. Return the pine nuts to the pan.

**5** Drain the fettuccine, toss in the remaining olive oil and transfer to a warmed serving dish. Spoon the anchovy and spinach sauce over the fettuccine, toss lightly and serve at once.

# crab ravioli

## ingredients

### SERVES 4

6 spring onions

350 g/12 oz cooked crabmeat

2 tsp finely chopped
fresh root ginger

$1/8$–$1/4$ tsp chilli or Tabasco
sauce

700 g/1 lb 9 oz tomatoes,
peeled, deseeded and
coarsely chopped

1 garlic clove, finely chopped

1 tbsp white wine vinegar

1 quantity basic pasta dough
(see below)

plain flour, for dusting

1 egg, lightly beaten

2 tbsp double cream

salt

shredded spring onion,
to garnish

## pasta dough

200 g/7 oz plain flour, plus
extra for dusting

pinch of salt

2 eggs, lightly beaten

1 tbsp olive oil

## method

**1** To make the pasta dough, sift the flour into a food processor. Add the salt, eggs and olive oil and process until the dough begins to come together. Knead on a lightly floured board until smooth. Cover and let rest for 30 minutes.

**2** Thinly slice the spring onions, keeping the white and green parts separate. Mix the green spring onions, crabmeat, ginger and chilli sauce in a bowl. Cover and chill.

**3** Process the tomatoes in a food processor to a purée. Place the garlic, white spring onions and vinegar in a pan and add the puréed tomatoes. Bring to the boil, stirring, then simmer gently for 10 minutes. Remove from the heat.

**4** Thinly roll out half of the pasta dough on a lightly floured board. Cover with a tea towel and roll out the other half. Place small mounds of the filling in rows 4 cm/1$1/2$ inches apart on one sheet of dough and brush in between with beaten egg. Cover with the other half of dough. Press down between the mounds, cut into squares and let rest on a tea towel for 1 hour.

**5** Bring a large saucepan of lightly salted water to the boil. Add the ravioli, return to the boil and cook for 5 minutes. Remove with a slotted spoon and drain on kitchen paper. Meanwhile, gently heat the tomato sauce and whisk in the cream. Serve the ravioli with the sauce poured over and garnished with shredded spring onion.

# spaghetti with clams

## ingredients

SERVES 4

1 kg/2 lb 4 oz live clams,
    scrubbed under cold
    running water*
175 ml/6 fl oz water
175 ml/6 fl oz dry white wine
350 g/12 oz dried spaghetti
5 tbsp olive oil
2 garlic cloves, finely chopped
4 tbsp chopped fresh
    flat-leaf parsley
salt and pepper

* discard any clams with
broken or damaged shells
and any that do not shut
when sharply tapped

## method

**1** Place the clams in a large, heavy-based saucepan, add the water and wine, cover and cook over high heat, shaking the pan occasionally, for 5 minutes, or until the shells have opened.

**2** Remove the clams with a slotted spoon and cool slightly. Strain the cooking liquid, through a sieve lined with cheesecloth, into a small pan. Bring to the boil and cook until reduced by about half, then remove from the heat. Meanwhile, discard any clams that have not opened, remove the remainder from their shells and reserve until required.

**3** Bring a large saucepan of lightly salted water to the boil. Add the pasta, return to the boil and cook for 8–10 minutes, or until tender but still firm to the bite.

**4** Meanwhile, heat the olive oil in a large, heavy-based frying pan. Add the garlic and cook, stirring frequently, for 2 minutes. Add the parsley and the reduced clam cooking liquid and simmer gently.

**5** Drain the pasta and add it to the frying pan with the clams. Season with salt and pepper and cook, stirring constantly, for 4 minutes, or until the pasta is coated and the clams have heated through. Transfer to a warmed serving dish and serve immediately.

# tagliatelle & mussels with white wine, garlic & parsley

## ingredients

### SERVES 4

2 kg/4 lb 8 oz mussels,
    scrubbed

1 large onion, chopped

3 garlic cloves, minced

550 ml/18 fl oz dry white wine

1 bay leaf

2 sprigs of fresh thyme

5 tbsp chopped fresh flat-leaf
    parsley

1 tbsp chopped fresh rosemary

4 tbsp butter

salt and pepper

450 g/1 lb dried tagliatelle or
    other broad-ribboned pasta

## method

**1** Clean the mussels by scrubbing the shells and pulling out any beards that are attached. Rinse well, discarding any with broken shells or that remain open when tapped.

**2** Put the onion, garlic, white wine, herbs and 2 tablespoons of the butter in a saucepan. Bring to the boil, then reduce the heat. Add the mussels, then season with salt and pepper. Cover and cook over medium heat for 3–4 minutes, shaking the pan, until the mussels open. Remove from the heat. Lift out the mussels with a perforated spoon, reserving the liquid. Discard any that remain closed. Remove most of the others from their shells, reserving a few in their shells to garnish.

**3** Cook the pasta until tender but still firm to the bite, then drain it and divide it between 4 individual serving bowls. Spoon the mussels over the pasta. Strain the mussel liquid and return to the pan. Add the remaining butter and heat until melted. Pour over the pasta, garnish with the mussels in their shells and serve immediately.

# mixed shellfish with angel-hair pasta

## ingredients

**SERVES 4**

85 g/3 oz prepared squid

1 tsp cornstarch

1 tbsp water

1 egg white

4 prepared scallops, sliced

85 g/3 oz raw prawns, shelled and deveined

salt

350 g/12 oz angel-hair pasta

3 tbsp peanut oil

55 g/2 oz mangetout

1 tbsp dark soy sauce

1 tbsp dry sherry

$1/2$ tsp light brown sugar

2 spring onions, shredded

## method

**1** Open out the squid and, with a sharp knife, score the inside with criss-cross lines. Cut into small pieces, about 2-cm/3/4-inch square. Place in a bowl and cover with boiling water. When the squares have curled up, drain and rinse in cold water. Mix the cornstarch and water together in a small bowl until a smooth paste forms and stir in about half the egg white. Add the scallops and prawns and toss until well coated.

**2** Bring a large heavy-based saucepan of lightly salted water to the boil. Add the pasta, return to the boil and cook for 5 minutes, or until tender but still firm to the bite.

**3** Meanwhile, heat the oil in a preheated wok or heavy-based frying pan. Add the mangetout, squid, scallops and prawns and stir-fry for 2 minutes. Stir in the soy sauce, sherry, sugar and spring onions and cook, stirring, for 1 minute. Drain the pasta and divide it between 4 warmed plates. Top with the shellfish mixture and serve at once.

# spaghetti & shellfish

## ingredients

**SERVES 4**

225 g/8 oz dried short-cut
  spaghetti, or long
  spaghetti broken into
  15-cm/6-inch lengths
1 tbsp olive oil
300 ml/10 fl oz chicken stock
1 tsp lemon juice
1 small cauliflower,
  cut into florets
2 carrots, sliced thinly
125 g/4$^1$/$_2$ oz mangetout
55 g/2 oz butter
1 onion, sliced
225 g/8 oz courgettes,
  thinly sliced
1 garlic clove, chopped
350 g/12 oz frozen shelled
  prawns, thawed
salt and pepper
2 tbsp chopped fresh parsley
25 g/1 oz freshly grated
  Parmesan cheese
$^1$/$_2$ tsp paprika, to sprinkle
4 unshelled prawns, to
  garnish (optional)
crusty bread, to serve

## method

**1** Bring a large, heavy-based saucepan
of lightly salted water to the boil. Add the
spaghetti, return to the boil and cook for 8–10
minutes, or until tender but still firm to the
bite. Drain, then return to the pan and stir in
the olive oil. Cover and keep warm.

**2** Bring the chicken stock and lemon juice to
the boil. Add the cauliflower and carrots and
cook for 3–4 minutes, until they are tender.
Remove with a slotted spoon and set aside.
Add the mangetout and cook for 1–2 minutes,
until they start to soften. Remove and add to
the other vegetables. Reserve the stock for
future use.

**3** Melt half of the butter in a frying pan over
medium heat and cook the onion and
courgettes for 3 minutes. Add the garlic and
prawns and cook for a further 2–3 minutes,
until thoroughly heated through.

**4** Stir in the reserved vegetables and heat
through. Season with salt and pepper, then
stir in the remaining butter. Transfer the
spaghetti to a warmed serving dish. Pour
on the sauce and parsley. Toss well using
2 forks, until thoroughly coated. Sprinkle on
the grated cheese and paprika and garnish
with unshelled prawns, if using. Serve at once,
with crusty bread.

# spaghetti with prawns

## ingredients

**SERVES 4**

450 g/1 lb dried spaghetti

125 ml/4 fl oz olive oil

6 garlic cloves, sliced thinly

450 g/1 lb raw medium
    prawns, shelled and
    deveined

2 tbsp flat-leaf parsley,
    chopped finely, plus
    2 tbsp extra, to garnish

125 ml/4 fl oz dry white wine

4 tbsp freshly squeezed
    lemon juice

salt and pepper

## method

**1** Bring a large saucepan of salted water to the boil over high heat. Add the spaghetti, return the water to the boil and boil for 10 minutes, or until tender.

**2** Meanwhile, heat the oil in another large saucepan over medium heat. Add the garlic and cook until just golden brown. Add the prawns and 2 tablespoons of chopped parsley and stir. Add the wine and simmer for 2 minutes. Stir in the lemon juice and simmer until the prawns turn pink and curl.

**3** Drain the spaghetti, then tip it into the pan with the prawns and toss. Season with salt and pepper.

**4** Transfer to a large serving platter and sprinkle with the extra parsley. Serve at once.

# seafood pasta pockets

## ingredients

### SERVES 4

2 tbsp virgin olive oil

2 fresh red chillies, deseeded
   and finely chopped

4 garlic cloves, finely chopped

800 g/1 lb 12 oz canned
   tomatoes

225 ml/8 fl oz dry white wine

salt and pepper

350 g/12 oz dried spaghetti

2 tbsp butter

115 g/4 oz prepared raw squid,
   sliced

175 g/6 oz raw jumbo prawns

450 g/1 lb live mussels,
   scrubbed and debearded*

1 crab, about 1.5 kg/3 lb 5 oz,
   freshly cooked, all meat
   removed

3 tbsp coarsely chopped
   fresh flat-leaf parsley

1 tbsp shredded fresh basil
   leaves

* discard any damaged
mussels or any that do not
shut immediately when
tapped; once cooked,
discard any mussels that
remain closed

## method

**1** Heat 1 tablespoon of the olive oil in a large pan. Add half the chillies and half the garlic and cook over medium heat, stirring occasionally, for 2–3 minutes. Add the tomatoes with their can juices and the wine. Reduce the heat and simmer for about 1 hour. Strain the sauce, season and set aside.

**2** Bring a saucepan of salted water to the boil. Add the pasta, return to the boil and cook for 10 minutes, until tender but still firm to the bite.

**3** Heat the remaining olive oil with the butter in a large, heavy-based saucepan. Add the remaining chilli and garlic and cook over low heat, stirring occasionally, for 5 minutes, or until softened. Add the squid, prawns and mussels, cover the pan and cook over high heat for 4–5 minutes, or until the mussels have opened. Remove the pan from the heat and stir in the crab meat.

**4** Drain the pasta and add it to the seafood with the chilli and tomato sauce, parsley, and basil, tossing well to coat.

**5** Cut out 4 large squares of baking parchment. Divide the pasta and seafood between them, placing it on one half. Fold over the other half and turn in the edges securely to seal. Transfer to a baking sheet and bake in a preheated oven, 180°C/350°F/Gas Mark 5, for 10 minutes, or until the pockets have puffed up. Serve at once.

# spaghetti with prawns & garlic sauce

## ingredients

**SERVES 4**

3 tbsp olive oil

3 tbsp butter

4 garlic cloves, minced

2 tbsp finely diced red pepper

2 tbsp tomato purée

125 ml/4 fl oz dry white wine

450 g/1 lb spaghetti or tagliatelle

350 g/12 oz raw shelled prawns

125 ml/4 fl oz double cream

salt and pepper

3 tbsp chopped fresh flat-leaf parsley, to garnish

## method

**1** Heat the oil and butter in a saucepan over medium–low heat. Add the garlic and red pepper. Fry for a few seconds until the garlic is just beginning to colour. Stir in the tomato purée and wine. Cook for 10 minutes, stirring.

**2** Cook the spaghetti in plenty of boiling salted water until tender but still firm to the bite. Drain and return to the saucepan.

**3** Add the prawns to the sauce and raise the heat to medium–high. Cook for 2 minutes, stirring, until the prawns turn pink. Reduce the heat and stir in the cream. Cook for 1 minute, stirring constantly, until thickened. Season with salt and pepper.

**4** Transfer the spaghetti to a warmed serving dish and pour over the sauce. Sprinkle with the parsley. Toss well to mix and serve at once.

# springtime pasta

## ingredients

**SERVES 4**

2 tbsp lemon juice

4 baby globe artichokes

7 tbsp olive oil

2 shallots, finely chopped

2 garlic cloves, finely chopped

2 tbsp chopped fresh flat-leaf parsley

2 tbsp chopped fresh mint

350 g/12 oz dried rigatoni or other tubular pasta

2 tbsp unsalted butter

12 large raw prawns, shelled and deveined

salt and pepper

## method

**1** Fill a large bowl with cold water and add the lemon juice. Prepare the artichokes one at a time. Cut off the stems and trim away any tough outer leaves. Cut across the tops of the leaves. Slice in half lengthways and remove the central fibrous chokes, then cut lengthways into slices 5 mm/1/4 inch thick. Immediately place the slices in the bowl of acidulated water to prevent discolouration.

**2** Heat 5 tablespoons of the olive oil in a heavy-based frying pan. Drain the artichoke slices and pat dry with kitchen paper. Add them to the pan with the shallots, garlic, parsley and mint and cook over low heat, stirring frequently, for 10–12 minutes, or until tender.

**3** Meanwhile, bring a large saucepan of lightly salted water to the boil. Add the pasta, return to the boil and cook for 8–10 minutes, or until tender but still firm to the bite.

**4** Melt the butter in a frying pan, cut the prawns in half and add them to the pan. Cook, stirring occasionally, for 2–3 minutes, or until the prawns have changed colour. Season with salt and pepper.

**5** Drain the pasta and tip it into a bowl. Add the remaining olive oil and toss well. Add the artichoke mixture and the prawns and toss again. Serve immediately.

# tagliatelle with prawns, tomatoes, garlic & chilli

## ingredients

**SERVES 4**

4 tbsp olive oil

5 garlic cloves, chopped
very finely

400 g/14 oz canned chopped
tomatoes

1 fresh red chilli, deseeded
and chopped very finely

salt and pepper

450 g/1 lb dried tagliatelle
or spaghetti

350 g/12 oz raw shelled
prawns

2 tbsp chopped fresh flat-leaf
parsley, plus extra to
garnish

## method

**1** Heat 2 tablespoons of the oil and the garlic in a saucepan over a medium–low heat. Cook the garlic until just beginning to colour. Add the tomatoes and chilli. Bring to the boil, then simmer over medium–low heat for 30 minutes until the oil separates from the tomatoes. Season with salt and pepper.

**2** Cook the pasta in plenty of boiling salted water until tender but still firm to the bite. Drain and return to the saucepan.

**3** Heat the remaining oil in a frying pan over high heat. Add the prawns and stir-fry for 2 minutes until pink. Add the prawns to the tomato mixture. Stir in the parsley, then let simmer over low heat until bubbling.

**4** Transfer the pasta to a warmed serving dish. Pour the sauce over the pasta. Toss well to mix. Garnish with chopped parsley and serve immediately.

# fusilli with hot cajun seafood sauce

## ingredients

**SERVES 4**

550 ml/18 fl oz double cream

8 spring onions, sliced thinly

55 g/2 oz chopped fresh
flat-leaf parsley

1 tbsp chopped fresh thyme

$1/2$ tbsp pepper

$1/2$–1 tsp dried chilli flakes

1 tsp salt

450 g/1 lb dried fusilli or
tagliatelle

40 g/$1^1/_2$ oz freshly grated
Gruyère cheese

25 g/1 oz freshly grated
Parmesan cheese

2 tbsp olive oil

225 g/8 oz raw shelled
prawns

225 g/8 oz scallops, sliced

1 tbsp shredded fresh basil,
to serve

## method

**1** Heat the cream in a large saucepan over medium heat, stirring constantly. When almost boiling, reduce the heat and add the spring onions, parsley, thyme, pepper, chilli flakes and salt. Simmer for 7–8 minutes, stirring, until thickened. Remove from the heat.

**2** Cook the pasta in plenty of boiling salted water until tender but still firm to the bite. Drain and return to the saucepan. Add the cream mixture and the cheeses to the pasta. Toss over low heat until the cheeses have melted. Transfer to a warmed serving dish.

**3** Heat the oil in a large frying pan over medium–high heat. Add the prawns and scallops. Stir-fry for 2–3 minutes until the prawns have just turned pink.

**4** Pour the seafood over the pasta and toss well to mix. Sprinkle with the basil and serve at once.

# pasta with scallops & pine nuts

## ingredients

**SERVES 4**

400 g/14 oz long, hollow
    Greek macaroni or other
    short pasta
4 tbsp olive oil
1 garlic clove, chopped finely
25 g/1 oz pine nuts
8 large scallops, sliced
salt and pepper
2 tbsp chopped fresh basil
    leaves

## method

**1** Cook the macaroni in a large saucepan of boiling salted water for 10–12 minutes or as directed on the packet, until tender.

**2** About 5 minutes before the pasta is ready, heat the oil in a frying pan. Add the garlic and fry for 1–2 minutes until softened but not browned. Add the pine nuts and cook until browned. Stir in the scallops and cook until just opaque. Season with salt and pepper.

**3** When the pasta is cooked, drain and return to the saucepan. Add the scallops and the juices in the frying pan to the pasta and toss together. Serve at once, sprinkled with the chopped basil.

# fettuccine with scallops in porcini & cream sauce

## ingredients

**SERVES 4**

25 g/1 oz dried porcini
mushrooms

550 ml/18 fl oz hot water

3 tbsp olive oil

3 tbsp butter

350 g/12 oz scallops, sliced

2 garlic cloves, chopped
very finely

2 tbsp lemon juice

250 ml/9 fl oz double cream

salt and pepper

350 g/12 oz dried fettuccine
or pappardelle

2 tbsp chopped fresh flat-leaf
parsley, to serve

## method

**1** Put the porcini and hot water in a bowl and soak for 20 minutes. Strain the mushrooms, reserving the soaking water, and chop coarsely. Line a sieve with kitchen paper and strain the mushroom water into a bowl.

**2** Heat the oil and butter in a large frying pan over medium heat. Add the scallops and cook for 2 minutes until just golden. Add the garlic and mushrooms and stir-fry for 1 minute.

**3** Stir in the lemon juice, cream and 125ml/ 4 fl oz of the mushroom water. Bring to the boil, then simmer over medium heat for 2–3 minutes, stirring constantly, until the liquid is reduced by half. Season with salt and pepper. Remove from the heat.

**4** Cook the pasta in plenty of boiling salted water until tender but still firm to the bite. Drain and transfer to a warmed serving dish. Briefly reheat the sauce and pour over the pasta. Sprinkle with the parsley and toss well to mix. Serve at once.

# vegetarian

Vegetarian pasta dishes are so good that even non-vegetarians enjoy them and don't seem to notice the absence of meat!

One reason for this might be the irresistible combination of pasta, cream and cheese that goes into some of the tastiest vegetarian recipes. If you love Parmesan cheese, try the classic Fettuccine Alfredo, which is simple but absolutely sumptuous, and Farfalle with Cream & Parmesan, which has an attractive sprinkling of bright green petits pois. If you prefer the more robust nature of Gorgonzola, which goes wonderfully with pasta, choose Pipe Rigate with Gorgonzola Sauce, Tagliatelle with Asparagus & Gorgonzola Sauce or Fusilli with Gorgonzola & Mushroom Sauce – rich dishes for special occasions.

For everyday lunches and suppers, recipes that include plenty of vegetables are ideal. Pasta with Green Vegetables, Pasta with Spiced Leek, Butternut Squash & Cherry Tomatoes and Penne with Pepper & Goat's Cheese Sauce are delicious, vibrantly coloured dishes. If you favour a traditional tomato sauce, Spaghetti with Tomato, Garlic & Basil Sauce is the one for you.

Spinach, ricotta and pasta are another perfect partnership, so we have included a recipe for Spinach & Ricotta Ravioli, using a homemade spinach pasta dough. Try it!

# fettuccine alfredo

## ingredients

**SERVES 4**

25 g/1 oz butter

225 ml7 fl oz double cream

450 g/1 lb fresh fettuccine

1 tbsp olive oil

90 g/3$^1$/$_4$ oz freshly grated
    Parmesan cheese, plus
    extra to serve

pinch of freshly grated nutmeg

salt and pepper

fresh flat-leaf parsley sprigs,
    to garnish

## method

**1** Place the butter and 150 ml/5 fl oz of the cream in a large saucepan and bring the mixture to the boil over medium heat. Reduce the heat and simmer gently for about 1$^1$/$_2$ minutes, or until slightly thickened.

**2** Meanwhile, bring a large saucepan of lightly salted water to the boil. Add the fettuccine and oil, return to the boil and cook for 2–3 minutes until tender but still firm to the bite. Drain the fettuccine, return it to the pan and pour the sauce over it. Return the pan to low heat and toss the fettuccine in the sauce until coated.

**3** Add the remaining cream, the Parmesan cheese and nutmeg to the fettuccine mixture and season with salt and pepper. Toss thoroughly to coat while gently heating through.

**4** Transfer the fettuccine mixture to a warmed serving plate and garnish with parsley sprigs. Serve immediately, with extra grated Parmesan cheese.

# paglia e fieno
# with garlic crumbs

## ingredients

### SERVES 4

350 g/12 oz fresh white
    breadcrumbs

4 tbsp finely chopped fresh
    flat-leaf parsley

1 tbsp chopped fresh chives

2 tbsp finely chopped fresh
    sweet marjoram

3 tbsp olive oil, plus extra
    to serve

3–4 garlic cloves, finely
    chopped

55 g/2 oz pine nuts

salt and pepper

450 g/1 lb fresh paglia e fieno

55 g/2 oz freshly grated
    romano cheese, to serve

## method

**1** Mix the breadcrumbs, parsley, chives and
marjoram together in a small bowl. Heat the
olive oil in a large heavy-based frying pan.
Add the breadcrumb mixture and the garlic
and pine nuts, season with salt and pepper
and cook over low heat, stirring constantly, for
5 minutes, or until the breadcrumbs become
golden, but not crisp. Remove the pan from
the heat and cover to keep warm.

**2** Bring a large heavy-based saucepan of lightly
salted water to the boil. Add the pasta, return
to the boil and cook for 4–5 minutes, or until
tender but still firm to the bite.

**3** Drain the pasta and transfer to a warmed
serving dish. Drizzle with 2–3 tablespoons of
olive oil and toss to mix. Add the garlic
breadcrumbs and toss again. Serve
immediately with the grated romano cheese.

# fettuccine with ricotta

## ingredients

**SERVES 4**

350 g/12 oz dried fettuccine

3 tbsp unsalted butter

2 tbsp chopped fresh flat-leaf
    parsley, plus extra leaves
    to garnish

225 g/8 oz ricotta cheese

225 g/8 oz ground almonds

150 ml/5 fl oz soured cream

2 tbsp extra-virgin olive oil

125 ml/4 fl oz hot chicken
    stock

pinch of freshly grated nutmeg

salt and pepper

1 tbsp pine nuts

## method

**1** Bring a large heavy-based saucepan of lightly salted water to the boil. Add the pasta, return to the boil and cook for 8–10 minutes, or until tender but still firm to the bite. Drain well and return to the pan. Add the butter and chopped parsley and toss thoroughly to coat.

**2** Mix the ricotta, ground almonds and soured cream together in a bowl. Gradually stir in the olive oil, followed by the hot chicken stock. Season with nutmeg and pepper.

**3** Transfer the pasta to a warmed dish, pour over the sauce and toss. Sprinkle with pine nuts, garnish with parsley leaves and serve immediately.

# pasta with pesto

## ingredients

**SERVES 4**

450 g/1 lb dried tagliatelle
salt
fresh basil sprigs, to garnish

### pesto

2 garlic cloves
25 g/1 oz pine nuts
salt
115 g/4 oz fresh basil leaves
55 g/2 oz freshly grated
  Parmesan cheese
125 ml/4 fl oz olive oil

## method

**1** To make the pesto, put the garlic, pine nuts, a large pinch of salt and the basil into a mortar and pound to a paste with a pestle. Transfer to a bowl and gradually, with a wooden spoon, work in the Parmesan cheese followed by the olive oil, to make a thick, creamy sauce. Taste and adjust the seasoning if necessary.

**2** Alternatively, put the garlic, pine nuts and a large pinch of salt into a food processor or blender and process briefly. Add the basil leaves and process to a paste. With the motor still running, gradually add the olive oil. Scrape into a bowl and beat in the Parmesan cheese. Season with salt.

**3** Bring a large saucepan of lightly salted water to the boil. Add the pasta, return to the boil and cook for 8–10 minutes, or until tender but still firm to the bite. Drain the pasta well, return to the pan and toss with half the pesto, then divide between warmed serving plates and top with the remaining pesto. Garnish with basil sprigs and serve immediately.

# spaghetti olio e aglio

## ingredients

**SERVES 4**

450 g/1 lb dried spaghetti

125 ml/4 fl oz extra-virgin
    olive oil

3 garlic cloves, finely chopped

salt and pepper

3 tbsp chopped fresh flat-leaf
    parsley

## method

**1** Bring a large, heavy-based saucepan of lightly salted water to the boil. Add the spaghetti, return to the boil and cook for 8–10 minutes, or until tender but still firm to the bite.

**2** Meanwhile, heat the olive oil in a heavy-based frying pan. Add the garlic and a pinch of salt and cook over low heat, stirring constantly, for 3–4 minutes, or until golden. Do not allow the garlic to brown or it will taste bitter. Remove the pan from the heat.

**3** Drain the pasta and transfer to a warmed serving dish. Pour in the garlic-flavoured olive oil, then add the chopped parsley and season with salt and pepper. Toss well and serve immediately.

# farfalle with cream & parmesan

## ingredients

**SERVES 4**

450 g/1 lb dried farfalle

2 tbsp unsalted butter

350 g/12 oz petits pois

200 ml/7 fl oz double cream

pinch of freshly grated nutmeg

salt and pepper

55 g/2 oz freshly grated
    Parmesan cheese,
    plus extra to serve

fresh flat-leaf parsley sprigs,
    to garnish

crusty bread, to serve

## method

**1** Bring a large saucepan of lightly salted water to the boil. Add the pasta, return to the boil and cook for 8–10 minutes, or until tender but still firm to the bite, then drain thoroughly.

**2** Melt the butter in a large, heavy-based saucepan. Add the petits pois and cook for 2–3 minutes. Add 150 ml/5 fl oz of the cream and bring to the boil. Reduce the heat and simmer for 1 minute, or until slightly thickened.

**3** Add the drained pasta to the cream mixture. Place the pan over low heat and toss until the farfalle are thoroughly coated. Season with nutmeg, salt and pepper, then add the remaining cream and the grated Parmesan cheese. Toss again and transfer to individual serving bowls. Garnish with parsley sprigs and serve immediately with extra Parmesan cheese, for sprinkling, and crusty bread.

# pipe rigate
# with gorgonzola sauce

## ingredients

**SERVES 4**

400 g/14 oz dried pipe rigate,
    rigatoni, or penne
2 tbsp unsalted butter
6 fresh sage leaves
200 g/7 oz Gorgonzola cheese,
    diced
175–225 ml/6–8 fl oz double
    cream
2 tbsp dry vermouth
salt and pepper

## method

**1** Bring a large heavy-based saucepan of lightly salted water to the boil. Add the pasta, return to the boil and cook for 8–10 minutes, until tender but still firm to the bite.

**2** Meanwhile, melt the butter in a separate heavy-based saucepan. Add the sage leaves and cook, stirring gently, for 1 minute. Remove and reserve the sage leaves. Add the cheese and cook, stirring constantly, over low heat until it has melted. Gradually, stir in 175 ml/6 fl oz of the cream and the vermouth. Season with salt and pepper and cook, stirring, until thickened. Add more cream if the sauce seems too thick.

**3** Drain the pasta well and transfer to a warmed serving dish. Add the Gorgonzola sauce, toss well to mix and serve at once, garnished with the reserved sage leaves.

# pasta with green vegetables

## ingredients

**SERVES 4**

225 g/8 oz dried gemelli or
    other pasta shapes
2 tbsp chopped fresh parsley
2 tbsp freshly grated
    Parmesan cheese

### sauce

1 head of broccoli,
    cut into florets
2 courgettes, sliced
225 g/8 oz asparagus,
    trimmed
125 g/4$^{1}$/$_{2}$ oz mangetout
125 g/4$^{1}$/$_{2}$ oz frozen peas
25 g/1 oz butter
3 tbsp vegetable stock
5 tbsp double cream
salt and pepper
large pinch of freshly grated
    nutmeg

## method

**1** Bring a large, heavy-based saucepan of lightly salted water to the boil. Add the pasta, return to the boil and cook for 8–10 minutes, or until tender but still firm to the bite. Drain the pasta, return to the pan, cover and keep warm.

**2** Steam the broccoli, courgettes, asparagus and mangetout over a pan of boiling, salted water until just beginning to soften. Remove from the heat and plunge into cold water to prevent further cooking. Drain and reserve. Cook the peas in boiling, salted water for 3 minutes, then drain. Refresh in cold water and drain again.

**3** Place the butter and vegetable stock in a saucepan over medium heat. Add all the vegetables except for the asparagus and toss carefully with a wooden spoon to heat through, taking care not to break them up. Stir in the cream, let the sauce heat through and season with salt, pepper and nutmeg.

**4** Transfer the pasta to a warmed serving dish and stir in the chopped parsley. Spoon the sauce over and sprinkle on the freshly grated Parmesan cheese. Arrange the asparagus in a pattern on top. Serve immediately.

# tagliatelle with asparagus & gorgonzola sauce

## ingredients

**SERVES 4**

450 g/1 lb asparagus tips

olive oil

salt and pepper

225 g/8 oz Gorgonzola,
    crumbled

175 ml/6 fl oz double cream

350 g/12 oz dried tagliatelle

## method

**1** Place the asparagus tips in a single layer in a shallow ovenproof dish. Sprinkle with a little olive oil and season with salt and pepper. Turn to coat in the oil and seasoning. Roast in a preheated oven, 230°C/450°F/Gas Mark 8, for 10–12 minutes, until slightly browned and just tender. Set aside and keep warm.

**2** Combine the crumbled cheese with the cream in a bowl. Season with salt and pepper.

**3** Cook the pasta in plenty of boiling salted water until tender but still firm to the bite. Drain and transfer to a warmed serving dish.

**4** Immediately add the asparagus and the cheese mixture. Toss well until the cheese has melted and the pasta is coated with the sauce. Serve at once.

# radiatore with pumpkin sauce

## ingredients

**SERVES 4**

4 tbsp unsalted butter

115 g/4 oz white onions or
  shallots, very finely chopped

800 g/1 lb 12 oz pumpkin,
  unprepared weight

pinch of freshly grated nutmeg

350 g/12 oz dried radiatore

200 ml/7 fl oz single cream

4 tbsp freshly grated
  Parmesan cheese,
  plus extra to serve

2 tbsp chopped fresh flat-leaf
  parsley

salt and pepper

## method

**1** Melt the butter in a heavy-based saucepan over low heat. Add the onions, sprinkle with a little salt, cover and cook, stirring frequently, for 25–30 minutes.

**2** Scoop out and discard the seeds from the pumpkin. Peel and finely chop the flesh. Tip the pumpkin into the pan and season with nutmeg. Cover and cook over low heat, stirring occasionally, for 45 minutes.

**3** Meanwhile, bring a large saucepan of lightly salted water to the boil. Add the pasta, return to the boil and cook for 8–10 minutes, or until tender but still firm to the bite. Drain thoroughly, reserving about 150 ml/5 fl oz of the cooking liquid.

**4** Stir the cream, grated Parmesan cheese and parsley into the pumpkin sauce and season with salt and pepper. If the mixture seems too thick, add some or all of the reserved cooking liquid and stir. Tip in the pasta and toss for 1 minute. Serve at once, with extra Parmesan cheese for sprinkling.

# pasta with spiced leek, butternut squash & cherry tomatoes

## ingredients

### SERVES 4

150 g/5¹/₂ oz baby leeks, cut
    into 2-cm/³/₄-inch slices
175 g/6 oz butternut squash,
    deseeded and cut into
    2-cm/³/₄-inch chunks
1¹/₂ tbsp medium curry paste
1 tsp vegetable oil
175 g/6 oz cherry tomatoes
250 g/9 oz dried pasta
    shapes
2 tbsp chopped fresh
    coriander leaves

### white sauce

250 ml/9 fl oz skimmed milk
20 g/³/₄ oz cornflour
1 tsp mustard powder
1 small onion, left whole
2 small bay leaves
4 tsp grated Parmesan
    cheese

## method

**1** To make the white sauce, put the milk into a saucepan with the flour, mustard, onion and bay leaves. Whisk over medium heat until thick. Remove from the heat, discard the onion and bay leaves and stir in the cheese. Set aside, stirring occasionally to prevent a skin forming.

**2** Bring a large saucepan of water to the boil, add the leeks and cook for 2 minutes. Add the butternut squash and cook for a further 2 minutes. Drain in a colander.

**3** Mix the curry paste with the oil in a large bowl. Toss the leeks and butternut squash in the mixture to coat thoroughly.

**4** Transfer the leeks and butternut squash to a non-stick baking sheet and roast in a preheated oven, 200°C/400°F/Gas Mark 6, for 10 minutes until golden brown. Add the tomatoes and roast for a further 5 minutes.

**5** Meanwhile, cook the pasta according to the instructions on the packet and drain.

**6** Put the white sauce into a large saucepan and warm over low heat. Add the leeks, butternut squash, tomatoes and coriander and stir in the warm pasta. Mix well and serve.

# spaghetti with tomato, garlic & basil sauce

## ingredients

**SERVES 4**

5 tbsp extra-virgin olive oil

1 onion, chopped finely

800 g/1 lb 12 oz canned
    chopped tomatoes

4 garlic cloves, cut into
    quarters

salt and pepper

450 g/1 lb dried spaghetti

large handful fresh basil
    leaves, shredded

freshly Parmesan cheese
    shavings, to serve

## method

**1** Heat the oil in a large saucepan over medium heat. Add the onion and fry gently for 5 minutes until soft. Add the tomatoes and garlic. Bring to the boil, then simmer over medium–low heat for 25–30 minutes until the oil separates from the tomato. Season with salt and pepper.

**2** Cook the pasta in plenty of boiling salted water until tender but still firm to the bite. Drain and transfer to a warmed serving dish.

**3** Pour the sauce over the pasta. Add the basil and toss well to mix. Serve with the Parmesan cheese shavings.

# fusilli with herbed sun-dried tomato sauce

## ingredients

**SERVES 4**

85 g/3 oz sun-dried tomatoes
   (not in oil)

750 ml/24 fl oz boiling water

2 tbsp olive oil

1 onion, chopped finely

2 large garlic cloves, sliced
   finely

2 tbsp chopped fresh flat-leaf
   parsley

2 tsp chopped fresh oregano

1 tsp chopped fresh rosemary

salt and pepper

350 g/12 oz dried fusilli

10 fresh basil leaves,
   shredded and 3 tbsp
   freshly grated Parmesan
   cheese, to serve

## method

**1** Put the tomatoes and boiling water in a bowl and let stand for 5 minutes. Using a perforated spoon, remove one third of the tomatoes from the bowl. Cut into bite-size pieces. Put the remaining tomatoes and water into a blender and purée.

**2** Heat the oil in a large frying pan over medium heat. Add the onion and gently fry for 5 minutes until soft. Add the garlic and fry until just beginning to colour. Add the puréed tomato and the reserved tomato pieces to the pan. Bring to the boil, then simmer over medium–low heat for 10 minutes. Stir in the herbs and season with salt and pepper. Simmer for 1 minute, then remove from the heat.

**3** Cook the pasta in plenty of boiling salted water, until tender but still firm to the bite. Drain and transfer to a warmed serving dish. Briefly reheat the sauce. Pour over the pasta, add the basil and toss well to mix. Sprinkle with the Parmesan cheese and serve at once.

# hot chilli pasta

## ingredients

### SERVES 4

150 ml/5 fl oz dry white wine

1 tbsp sun-dried tomato
   purée

2 fresh red chillies

2 garlic cloves, finely chopped

350 g/12 oz dried tortiglioni

4 tbsp chopped fresh flat-leaf
   parsley

fresh romano cheese
   shavings, to garnish

### sugocasa

5 tbsp extra-virgin olive oil

450 g/1 lb plum tomatoes,
   chopped

salt and pepper

## method

**1** First make the sugocasa. Heat the olive oil in a frying pan until it is almost smoking. Add the tomatoes and cook over high heat for 2–3 minutes. Reduce the heat to low and cook gently for 20 minutes, or until very soft. Season with salt and pepper, then pass through a food mill or blender into a clean saucepan.

**2** Add the wine, sun-dried tomato purée, whole chillies and garlic to the sugocasa and bring to the boil. Reduce the heat and simmer gently.

**3** Meanwhile, bring a large pan of lightly salted water to the boil. Add the pasta, return to the boil and cook for 8–10 minutes, or until tender but still firm to the bite.

**4** Meanwhile, remove the chillies and taste the sauce. If you prefer a hotter flavour, chop some or all of the chillies and return them to the pan. Check the seasoning at the same time, then stir in half the parsley.

**5** Drain the pasta and tip it into a warmed serving bowl. Add the sauce and toss to coat. Sprinkle with the remaining parsley, garnish with the romano shavings and serve at once.

# chilli broccoli pasta

## ingredients

### SERVES 4

225 g/8 oz dried penne or
  macaroni

225 g/8 oz head of broccoli,
  cut into florets

50 ml/2 fl oz extra-virgin olive
  oil

2 large garlic cloves, chopped

2 fresh red chillies, deseeded
  and diced

8 cherry tomatoes (optional)

fresh basil leaves, to garnish

## method

**1** Bring a large saucepan of salted boiling water to the boil. Add the pasta, return to the boil and cook for 8–10 minutes until tender but still firm to the bite. Drain the pasta, refresh under cold running water and drain again. Set aside.

**2** Bring a separate saucepan of salted water to the boil, add the broccoli and cook for 5 minutes. Drain, refresh under cold running water and drain again.

**3** Heat the oil in the pan that the pasta was cooked in over high heat. Add the garlic, chillies and tomatoes, if using, and cook, stirring, for 1 minute.

**4** Add the broccoli and mix well. Cook for 2 minutes, stirring, to heat through. Add the pasta and mix well again. Cook for a further minute. Transfer the pasta to a large, warmed serving bowl and serve garnished with basil leaves.

# penne in a creamy mushroom sauce

## ingredients

### SERVES 4

55 g/2 oz butter

1 tbsp olive oil

6 shallots, sliced

450 g/1 lb chestnut
    mushrooms, sliced

salt and pepper

1 tsp plain flour

150 ml/5 fl oz double cream

2 tbsp port

115 g/4 oz sun-dried
    tomatoes in oil, drained
    and chopped

pinch freshly grated nutmeg

350 g/12 oz dried penne

2 tbsp chopped fresh flat-leaf
    parsley

## method

**1** Melt the butter with the olive oil in a large, heavy-based frying pan. Add the shallots and cook over low heat, stirring occasionally, for 4–5 minutes, or until softened. Add the mushrooms and cook over low heat for a further 2 minutes. Season with salt and pepper, sprinkle in the flour and cook, stirring, for 1 minute.

**2** Remove the pan from the heat and gradually stir in the cream and port. Return to the heat, add the sun-dried tomatoes and grated nutmeg and cook over low heat, stirring occasionally, for 8 minutes.

**3** Meanwhile, bring a large, heavy-based saucepan of lightly salted water to the boil. Add the pasta, return to the boil and cook for 8–10 minutes, or until tender but still firm to the bite. Drain the pasta well and add to the mushroom sauce. Cook for 3 minutes, then transfer to a warmed serving dish. Sprinkle with the chopped parsley and serve immediately.

# fusilli with gorgonzola & mushroom sauce

## ingredients

**SERVES 4**

350 g/12 oz dried fusilli

3 tbsp olive oil

350 g/12 oz wild mushrooms
or white mushrooms, sliced

1 garlic clove, finely chopped

400 ml/14 fl oz double cream

250 g/9 oz Gorgonzola cheese,
crumbled

salt and pepper

2 tbsp chopped fresh flat-leaf
parsley, to garnish

## method

**1** Bring a large saucepan of lightly salted water to the boil. Add the pasta, return to the boil and cook for 8–10 minutes, or until tender but still firm to the bite.

**2** Meanwhile, heat the olive oil in a heavy-based saucepan. Add the mushrooms and cook over low heat, stirring frequently, for 5 minutes. Add the garlic to the pan and cook for a further 2 minutes.

**3** Add the cream, bring to the boil and cook for 1 minute, until slightly thickened. Stir in the cheese and cook over low heat until it has melted. Do not allow the sauce to boil once the cheese has been added. Season with salt and pepper and remove the pan from the heat.

**4** Drain the pasta and tip it into the sauce. Toss well to coat, then serve immediately, garnished with the parsley.

# tagliatelle with roasted artichokes & horseradish-herb sauce

## ingredients

**SERVES 2**

100 g/3¹/₂ oz canned
    artichokes, cut into
    quarters

vegetable oil spray

50 g/1³/₄ oz fresh baby
    spinach leaves

100 g/3¹/₂ oz dried tagliatelle

100 ml/3¹/₂ fl oz white sauce
    (see page 162)

2 tsp chopped fresh basil,
    plus extra to garnish

1 tsp finely chopped fresh
    lemon thyme, plus extra
    to garnish

1 tsp creamed horseradish

2 tsp soured cream

## method

**1** Spread the artichokes out on a non-stick baking sheet, spray lightly with oil and roast in a preheated oven, 220°C/425°F/Gas Mark 7, for 20 minutes until golden brown.

**2** Meanwhile, heat a large, lidded saucepan over medium heat. Add the spinach, cover and steam for 2 minutes. Remove from the heat and drain the spinach in a colander.

**3** Cook the pasta according to the instructions on the packet and drain.

**4** Return the drained spinach to the pan, add the sauce and heat gently. Add the herbs, horseradish, soured cream and artichokes and stir in the warm pasta. Heat to warm through, then serve garnished with extra herbs.

# conchiglie with marinated artichoke, onion & tomato sauce

## ingredients

**SERVES 4**

280 g/10 oz bottled
    marinated artichoke hearts

3 tbsp olive oil

1 onion, chopped finely

3 garlic cloves, minced

1 tsp dried oregano

$^1/_4$ tsp dried chilli flakes

400 g/14 oz canned chopped
    tomatoes

salt and pepper

350 g/12 oz dried conchiglie

4 tsp freshly grated Parmesan
    cheese

3 tbsp chopped fresh flat-leaf
    parsley

## method

**1** Drain the artichoke hearts, reserving the marinade. Heat the oil in a large saucepan over medium heat. Add the onion and fry for 5 minutes until translucent. Add the garlic, oregano, chilli flakes and the reserved artichoke marinade. Cook for a further 5 minutes.

**2** Stir in the tomatoes. Bring to the boil, then simmer over medium–low heat for 30 minutes. Season generously with salt and pepper.

**3** Cook the pasta in plenty of boiling salted water until tender but still firm to the bite. Drain and transfer to a warmed serving dish.

**4** Add the artichokes, Parmesan cheese and parsley to the sauce. Cook for a few minutes until heated through. Pour the sauce over the pasta, toss well to mix and serve at once.

# fusilli with courgettes, lemon & rosemary sauce

## ingredients

**SERVES 4**

6 tbsp olive oil

1 small onion, sliced
   very thinly

2 garlic cloves, chopped
   very finely

2 tbsp chopped fresh
   rosemary

1 tbsp chopped fresh flat-leaf
   parsley

450 g/1 lb small courgettes,
   cut into 5-mm x 4-cm/
   $^1/_4$-inch x $1^1/_2$-inch strips

finely grated rind of 1 lemon

salt and pepper

450 g/1 lb fusilli tricolore

4 tbsp freshly grated
   Parmesan cheese

## method

**1** Heat the olive oil in a large frying pan over medium–low heat. Add the onion and gently fry, stirring occasionally, for about 10 minutes until golden.

**2** Raise the heat to medium–high. Add the garlic, rosemary and parsley and cook for a few seconds, stirring. Add the courgettes and lemon rind. Cook for 5–7 minutes, stirring occasionally, until the courgettes are just tender. Season with salt and pepper. Remove from the heat.

**3** Cook the pasta in plenty of boiling salted water until tender but still firm to the bite. Drain and transfer to a warmed serving dish.

**4** Briefly reheat the courgettes. Pour over the pasta and toss well to mix. Sprinkle with the Parmesan cheese and serve immediately.

# aubergines & pasta

## ingredients

### SERVES 4

150 ml/5 fl oz vegetable stock

150 ml/5 fl oz white wine
vinegar

2 tsp balsamic vinegar

3 tbsp olive oil

1 fresh oregano sprig

450 g/1 lb aubergines, peeled
and thinly sliced

400 g/14 oz dried linguine

### marinade

2 tbsp extra-virgin olive oil

2 garlic cloves, crushed

2 tbsp chopped fresh oregano

2 tbsp finely chopped roasted
almonds

2 tbsp diced red pepper

2 tbsp lime juice

grated rind and juice
of 1 orange

salt and pepper

## method

**1** Place the vegetable stock, wine vinegar and balsamic vinegar into a large, heavy-based saucepan and bring to the boil over low heat. Add 2 teaspoons of the olive oil and the oregano sprig, and simmer gently for 1 minute. Add the aubergine slices to the pan, remove from the heat and let stand for 10 minutes.

**2** Meanwhile, make the marinade. Mix the olive oil, garlic, fresh oregano, almonds, pepper, lime juice and orange rind and juice together in a large bowl, and season with salt and pepper.

**3** Carefully remove the aubergine from the pan with a slotted spoon, and drain well. Add the aubergine slices to the marinade, mixing well, and let marinate in the refrigerator for 12 hours.

**4** Bring a large, heavy-based saucepan of lightly salted water to the boil. Add half of the remaining olive oil and the linguine, return to the boil and cook for 8–10 minutes, or until just tender but still firm to the bite. Drain the pasta thoroughly and toss with the remaining olive oil while still warm. Arrange the pasta on a serving plate with the aubergine slices and the marinade. Serve immediately.

# tagliatelle with walnuts

## ingredients

### SERVES 4

25 g/1 oz fresh white
  breadcrumbs

350 g/12 oz walnut pieces

2 garlic cloves, finely chopped

4 tbsp milk

4 tbsp olive oil

85 g/3 oz cream cheese

150 ml/5 fl oz single cream

salt and pepper

350 g/12 oz dried tagliatelle

## method

1 Place the breadcrumbs, walnuts, garlic, milk, olive oil and cream cheese in a large mortar and grind to a smooth paste with a pestle. Alternatively, place the ingredients in a food processor and process until smooth. Stir in the cream to give a thick sauce consistency and season with salt and pepper. Set aside.

2 Bring a large heavy-based saucepan of lightly salted water to the boil. Add the pasta, return to the boil and cook for 8–10 minutes, or until tender but still firm to the bite.

3 Drain the pasta and transfer to a warmed serving dish. Add the walnut sauce and toss thoroughly to coat. Serve immediately.

# ziti with rocket

## ingredients

**SERVES 4**

350 g/12 oz dried ziti, broken
     into 4-cm/1$^1$/$_2$-inch lengths
5 tbsp extra-virgin olive oil
2 garlic cloves, lightly crushed
200 g/7 oz rocket
2 fresh red chillies,
     thickly sliced
fresh red chilli flowers,
     to garnish
freshly grated romano cheese,
     to serve

## method

**1** Bring a large, heavy-based saucepan of
lightly salted water to the boil. Add the pasta,
return to the boil and cook for 8–10 minutes,
or until tender but still firm to the bite.

**2** Meanwhile, heat the olive oil in a large,
heavy-based frying pan. Add the garlic, rocket
and chillies and stir-fry for 5 minutes, or until
the rocket has wilted.

**3** Stir 2 tablespoons of the pasta cooking water
into the rocket, then drain the pasta and add
to the frying pan. Cook, stirring frequently, for
2 minutes, then transfer to a warmed serving
dish. Remove and discard the garlic cloves
and chillies, garnish with red chilli flowers and
serve immediately with the romano cheese.

# pasta provençal

## ingredients

**SERVES 4**

225 g/8 oz dried penne

1 tbsp olive oil

salt and pepper

25 g/1 oz pitted black olives,
    drained and chopped

25 g/1 oz dry-pack sun-dried
    tomatoes, soaked, strained
    and chopped

400 g/14 oz canned artichoke
    hearts, strained and
    halved

115 g/4 oz baby courgettes,
    trimmed and sliced

115 g/4 oz baby plum
    tomatoes, halved

100 g/3$^1$/$_2$ oz assorted baby
    salad leaves

shredded basil leaves,
    to garnish

### dressing

4 tbsp canned crushed
    tomatoes

2 tbsp low-fat cream cheese

1 tbsp unsweetened orange
    juice

1 small bunch of fresh basil,
    shredded

## method

**1** Cook the pasta according to the packet instructions, or until tender but still firm to the bite. Drain well and return to the saucepan. Stir in the oil, salt, pepper, olives and sun-dried tomatoes. Set aside to cool.

**2** Gently mix the artichokes, courgettes and plum tomatoes into the cooked pasta.

**3** To make the dressing, mix all the ingredients together and toss into the vegetables and pasta.

**4** Arrange the salad leaves in a large serving bowl. Spoon the mixture on top of the salad leaves and garnish with shredded basil leaves.

# linguine with roasted garlic & red pepper sauce

## ingredients

**SERVES 4**

6 large garlic cloves, unpeeled

400 g/14 oz bottled roasted red peppers, strained and sliced

200 g/7 oz canned chopped tomatoes

3 tbsp olive oil

1/4 tsp dried chilli flakes

1 tsp chopped fresh thyme or oregano

salt and pepper

350 g/12 oz dried linguine, spaghetti or bucatini

freshly grated Parmesan cheese, to serve

## method

**1** Place the unpeeled garlic cloves in a shallow, ovenproof dish. Roast in a preheated oven, 200°C/400°F/Gas Mark 6, for 7–10 minutes until the cloves feel soft.

**2** Put the peppers, tomatoes and oil in a food processor or blender, then purée. Squeeze the garlic flesh into the purée. Add the chilli flakes and oregano. Season with salt and pepper. Blend again, then scrape into a saucepan and set aside.

**3** Cook the pasta in plenty of boiling salted water until tender but still firm to the bite. Drain and transfer to a warmed serving dish.

**4** Reheat the sauce and pour over the pasta. Toss well to mix. Serve at once with Parmesan cheese.

# penne with pepper & goat's cheese sauce

## ingredients

**SERVES 4**

2 tbsp olive oil

1 tbsp butter

1 small onion, chopped finely

4 peppers, yellow and red, deseeded and cut into 2-cm/$^3$/$_4$-inch squares

3 garlic cloves, sliced thinly

salt and pepper

450 g/1 lb dried penne or rigatoni

125 g/4$^1$/$_2$ oz goat's cheese, crumbled

15 fresh basil leaves, shredded

10 black olives, pitted and sliced

## method

**1** Heat the oil and butter in a large frying pan over medium heat. Add the onion and fry until soft. Raise the heat to medium–high and add the peppers and garlic. Cook for 12–15 minutes, stirring, until the peppers are just tender. Season with salt and pepper. Remove from the heat.

**2** Cook the pasta in plenty of boiling salted water until tender but still firm to the bite. Drain and transfer to a warmed serving dish. Add the goat's cheese and toss to mix.

**3** Briefly reheat the sauce. Add the basil and olives. Pour over the pasta and toss well to mix, then serve immediately.

# spinach & ricotta ravioli

## ingredients

**SERVES 4**

spinach pasta dough

225 g/8 oz spinach leaves

200 g/7 oz plain flour, plus extra for dusting

pinch of salt

2 eggs, lightly beaten

1 tbsp olive oil

filling

350 g/12 oz spinach leaves, coarse stalks removed

225 g/8 oz ricotta cheese

55 g/2 oz freshly grated Parmesan cheese, plus extra, to serve

2 eggs, lightly beaten

pinch of freshly grated nutmeg

pepper

plain flour, for dusting

## method

**1** To make the pasta dough, blanch the spinach in boiling water for 1 minute, then drain thoroughly and chop finely. Sift the flour into a food processor. Add the spinach, salt, eggs and olive oil and process until the dough begins to come together. Knead on a lightly floured board until smooth. Cover and let rest for 30 minutes.

**2** To make the filling, cook the spinach, with just the water clinging to the leaves after washing, over low heat for 5 minutes, or until wilted. Drain and squeeze out as much moisture as possible. Cool, then chop finely. Beat the ricotta cheese until smooth, then stir in the spinach, Parmesan cheese and half the egg and season with nutmeg and pepper.

**3** Halve the pasta dough. Roll out one half on a floured board. Cover, and roll out the other half. Put small mounds of filling in rows 4 cm/ 1 1/2 inches apart on one sheet of dough and brush in between with the remaining egg. Cover with the other half. Press down between the mounds, pushing out any air. Cut into squares and let rest on a tea towel for 1 hour.

**4** Bring a large saucepan of salted water to the boil, add the ravioli, in batches, return to the boil and cook for 5 minutes. Remove with a slotted spoon and drain on kitchen paper. Serve with grated Parmesan cheese.

# al forno
## (baked in the oven)

It's cold, it's wet, you're feeling miserable and you need cheering up – fast! A baked pasta dish is the answer. Layers of pasta and sauce with a cheese topping, pasta tubes stuffed with a delicious filling, or the ultimate comfort food, Macaroni Cheese, will chase away those blues. Resist the temptation to open the oven door while your favourite recipe is cooking – instead, enjoy the anticipation of that tastebud-tempting aroma as the finished dish emerges, piping hot and bubbling on top.

Lasagna is one of the best-loved pasta dishes – try a traditional Lasagna or Lasagna Verde, a Chicken Lasagna or a Marsala Mushroom Lasagna. For a seafood version, Lasagna alla Marinara is packed with prawns and monkfish, while Vegetarian Lasagna is layered with a tantalizing mix of chargrilled aubergines and courgettes fried with garlic and herbs.

Cannelloni is fun to make – large tubes of pasta stuffed with your favourite filling and baked in a sauce. Try Chicken & Wild Mushroom Cannelloni or Cannelloni with Spinach & Ricotta. Mixed Vegetable Agnolotti are stuffed half-circles of home-made pasta, cooked first in boiling water then finished off in the oven with a generous coating of Parmesan cheese. It comes with a feel-good guarantee!

# lasagna verde

## ingredients

**SERVES 4**

butter, for greasing

225 g/8 oz no-precook
    lasagna verde

300 ml/10 fl oz béchamel
    sauce (see page 230)

55 g/2 oz freshly grated
    Parmesan cheese

green salad, tomato salad or
    black olives, to serve

### meat sauce

3 tbsp olive oil

45 g/1$^1$/$_2$ oz butter

2 large onions, chopped

4 celery stalks, thinly sliced

175 g/6 oz bacon, chopped

2 garlic cloves, chopped

500 g/1 lb 2 oz fresh
    minced beef

2 tbsp tomato purée

1 tbsp plain flour

400 g/14 oz canned chopped
    tomatoes

150 ml/5 fl oz beef stock

150 ml/5 fl oz red wine

salt and pepper

2 tsp dried oregano

$^1$/$_2$ tsp freshly grated nutmeg

## method

**1** To make the meat sauce, heat the oil and butter in a large frying pan over medium heat. Add the onions, celery and bacon and fry for 5 minutes, stirring. Stir in the garlic and minced beef and cook, stirring, until the meat changes colour. Reduce the heat and cook for 10 minutes, stirring.

**2** Increase the heat to medium, stir in the tomato purée and the flour and cook for 1–2 minutes. Stir in the tomatoes, stock and wine and bring to the boil, stirring. Season with salt and pepper and stir in the oregano and nutmeg. Simmer uncovered, stirring, for 55 minutes–1 hour, or until the mixture is reduced to a thick paste.

**3** Spoon a little of the meat sauce into a greased rectangular ovenproof dish, cover with a layer of lasagna, then spoon over a little béchamel sauce. Continue making layers in this way, covering the final layer of lasagne with the remaining béchamel sauce.

**4** Sprinkle over the cheese and bake in a preheated oven, 190°C/375°F/Gas Mark 5, for 40 minutes, or until the sauce is golden brown and bubbling. Serve with a green salad, a tomato salad or a bowl of black olives.

# sicilian linguine

## ingredients

### SERVES 4

125 ml/4 fl oz olive oil, plus
extra for brushing

2 aubergines, sliced

350 g/12 oz fresh minced
beef

1 onion, chopped

2 garlic cloves, finely chopped

2 tbsp tomato purée

400 g/14 oz canned chopped
tomatoes

1 tsp Worcestershire sauce

1 tbsp chopped fresh flat-leaf
parsley

salt and pepper

55 g/2 oz pitted black olives,
sliced

1 red pepper, deseeded
and chopped

175 g/6 oz dried linguine

115 g/4 oz freshly grated
Parmesan cheese

## method

**1** Brush a 20-cm/8-inch loose-based round cake pan with oil and line the bottom with baking parchment. Heat half the oil in a frying pan. Add the aubergines in batches and cook until lightly browned on both sides. Add more oil, as required. Drain the aubergines on kitchen paper, then arrange in overlapping slices to cover the bottom and sides of the cake pan, reserving a few slices.

**2** Heat the remaining olive oil in a large saucepan and add the beef, onion and garlic. Cook over medium heat, breaking up the meat with a wooden spoon, until browned all over. Add the tomato purée, tomatoes and their can juices, Worcestershire sauce and parsley. Season with salt and pepper and simmer for 10 minutes. Add the olives and pepper and cook for 10 minutes.

**3** Meanwhile, bring a saucepan of lightly salted water to the boil. Add the pasta, return to the boil and cook for 8–10 minutes, or until tender but still firm to the bite. Drain and transfer to a bowl. Add the meat sauce and cheese and toss, then spoon into the cake pan, press down and cover with the remaining aubergine slices. Bake in a preheated oven, 200°C/400°F/Gas Mark 6, for 40 minutes. Remove from the oven and let stand for 5 minutes, then loosen round the edges and invert onto a plate. Remove and discard the baking parchment and serve.

# lasagna

## ingredients

### SERVES 4

3 tbsp olive oil

1 onion, finely chopped

1 celery stalk, finely chopped

1 carrot, finely chopped

100 g/3¹/2 oz pancetta or
    rindless lean bacon,
    finely chopped

175 g/6 oz minced beef

175 g/6 oz minced pork

50 ml/2 fl oz dry red wine

150 ml/5 fl oz beef stock

1 tbsp tomato purée

salt and pepper

1 clove

1 bay leaf

150 ml/5 fl oz boiling milk

4 tbsp unsalted butter, diced,
    plus extra for greasing

400 g/14 oz dried
    no-precook lasagna

300 ml/10 fl oz béchamel
    sauce (see page 230)

140 g/5 oz mozzarella
    cheese, diced

140 g/5 oz freshly grated
    Parmesan cheese

## method

**1** Heat the olive oil in a large, heavy-based saucepan. Add the onion, celery, carrot, pancetta, beef and pork and cook over medium heat, stirring frequently and breaking up the meat with a wooden spoon, for 10 minutes, or until lightly browned.

**2** Add the wine, bring to the boil and cook until reduced. Add about two thirds of the stock, bring to the boil and cook until reduced. Combine the remaining stock and tomato purée and add to the pan. Season with salt and pepper, add the clove and bay leaf and pour in the milk. Cover and simmer over low heat for 1¹/2 hours. Remove from the heat and discard the clove and bay leaf.

**3** Lightly grease a large, ovenproof dish with butter. Place a layer of lasagna in the bottom and cover it with a layer of meat sauce. Spoon a layer of béchamel sauce on top and sprinkle with one third of the mozzarella and Parmesan cheeses. Continue making layers until all the ingredients are used, ending with a topping of béchamel sauce and sprinkled cheese.

**4** Dot the top of the lasagna with the diced butter and bake in a preheated oven, 200°C/400°F/Gas Mark 6, for 30 minutes, or until golden and bubbling.

# pork & pasta casserole

## ingredients

**SERVES 4**

2 tbsp olive oil

1 onion, chopped

1 garlic clove, finely chopped

2 carrots, diced

55 g/2 oz pancetta or rindless
 lean bacon, chopped

115 g/4 oz mushrooms,
 chopped

450 g/1 lb minced pork

125 ml/4 fl oz dry white wine

4 tbsp strained canned
 tomatoes

200 g/7 oz canned chopped
 tomatoes

2 tsp chopped fresh sage or
 $\frac{1}{2}$ tsp dried sage

salt and pepper

225 g/8 oz dried elicoidali

140 g/5 oz mozzarella cheese,
 diced

4 tbsp freshly grated
 Parmesan cheese

300 ml/10 fl oz béchamel
 sauce (see page 230)

## method

**1** Heat the olive oil in a large, heavy-based
frying pan. Add the onion, garlic and carrots
and cook over low heat, stirring occasionally,
for 5 minutes, or until the onion has softened.
Add the pancetta and cook for 5 minutes.
Add the chopped mushrooms and cook,
stirring occasionally, for a further 2 minutes.
Add the pork and cook, breaking it up with a
wooden spoon, until the meat is browned all
over. Stir in the wine, strained tomatoes,
chopped tomatoes and their can juices and
sage. Season with salt and pepper and bring
to the boil, then cover and simmer over low
heat for 25–30 minutes.

**2** Meanwhile, bring a large, heavy-based
saucepan of lightly salted water to the boil.
Add the pasta, return to the boil and cook for
8–10 minutes, or until tender but still firm to
the bite.

**3** Spoon the pork mixture into a large
ovenproof dish. Stir the mozzarella and half the
Parmesan cheese into the béchamel sauce.
Drain the pasta and stir the sauce into it, then
spoon it over the pork mixture. Sprinkle with
the remaining Parmesan cheese and bake in
a preheated oven, 200°C/400°F/Gas Mark 6,
for 25–30 minutes, or until golden brown.
Serve at once.

# cannelloni with ham & ricotta

## ingredients

**SERVES 4**

2 tbsp olive oil

2 onions, chopped

2 garlic cloves, finely chopped

1 tbsp shredded fresh basil

800 g/1 lb 12 oz chopped tomatoes

1 tbsp tomato purée

salt and pepper

350 g/12 oz dried cannelloni tubes

butter, for greasing

225 g/8 oz ricotta cheese

115 g/4 oz cooked ham, diced

1 egg

55 g/2 oz freshly grated romano cheese

## method

**1** Heat the olive oil in a large, heavy-based frying pan. Add the onions and garlic and cook over low heat, stirring occasionally, for 5 minutes, or until the onion is softened. Add the basil, chopped tomatoes and their can juices and tomato purée and season with salt and pepper. Reduce the heat and simmer for 30 minutes, or until thickened.

**2** Meanwhile, bring a large, heavy-based saucepan of lightly salted water to the boil. Add the dried cannelloni tubes, return to the boil and cook for 8–10 minutes, or until tender but still firm to the bite. Using a slotted spoon, transfer the cannelloni tubes to a large plate and pat dry with kitchen paper.

**3** Grease a large, shallow ovenproof dish with butter. Mix the ricotta, ham and egg together in a bowl and season with salt and pepper. Using a teaspoon, fill the cannelloni tubes with the ricotta, ham and egg mixture and place in a single layer in the dish. Pour the tomato sauce over the cannelloni and sprinkle with the grated romano cheese. Bake in a preheated oven, 180°C/350°F/Gas Mark 4, for 30 minutes, or until golden brown. Serve at once.

# pasticcio

## ingredients

**SERVES 4**

1 tbsp olive oil

1 onion, chopped

2 garlic cloves, finely chopped

450 g/1 lb fresh minced lamb

2 tbsp tomato purée

2 tbsp plain flour

300 ml/10 fl oz chicken stock

salt and pepper

1 tsp ground cinnamon

115 g/4 oz dried short-cut
    macaroni

2 beefsteak tomatoes, sliced

300 ml/10 fl oz Greek-style
    yogurt

2 eggs, lightly beaten

## method

**1** Heat the olive oil in a large heavy-based
frying pan. Add the onion and garlic and
cook over low heat, stirring occasionally, for
5 minutes, or until softened. Add the lamb
and cook, breaking it up with a wooden spoon,
until browned all over. Add the tomato purée
and sprinkle in the flour. Cook, stirring, for
1 minute, then stir in the chicken stock.
Season with salt and pepper and stir in the
cinnamon. Bring to the boil, reduce the heat,
cover and cook for 25 minutes.

**2** Meanwhile, bring a large heavy-based
saucepan of lightly salted water to the boil.
Add the pasta, return to the boil and cook for
8–10 minutes, or until tender but still firm to
the bite.

**3** Spoon the lamb mixture into a large
ovenproof dish and arrange the tomato
slices on top. Drain the pasta and transfer to
a bowl. Add the yogurt and eggs and mix well.
Spoon the pasta mixture on top of the lamb
and bake in a preheated oven, 190°C/375°F/
Gas Mark 5, for 1 hour. Serve immediately.

# chicken cannelloni

## ingredients

**SERVES 4**

4 skinless, boneless chicken
    breasts, diced

2 tbsp olive oil

6 tbsp butter

550 ml/18 fl oz double cream

1 tsp salt

1 tsp pepper

1/4 tsp freshly grated nutmeg

55 g/2 oz freshly grated
    Parmesan cheese

450 g/1 lb ricotta cheese

1 egg, lightly beaten

1 tbsp chopped fresh oregano

2 tbsp chopped fresh basil

225 g/8 oz dried cannelloni

75 g/2³/4 oz mozzarella cheese,
    freshly grated

fresh basil sprigs, to garnish

marinade

125 ml/4 fl oz white wine
    vinegar

1 garlic clove, crushed

125 ml/4 fl oz olive oil

## method

**1** To make the marinade, mix the vinegar,
garlic and olive oil together in a large bowl.
Add the chicken, cover with clingfilm and
marinate for 30 minutes.

**2** Heat the 2 tablespoons of olive oil in a frying
pan. Drain the chicken and cook for 5–7
minutes, stirring, until it turns white. Set aside.

**3** Melt the butter in a saucepan over medium–
high heat. Add the cream, salt, pepper and
nutmeg. Stir until thickened. Reduce the heat,
add the Parmesan cheese and stir until melted.
Remove from the heat.

**4** Mix the ricotta, egg and herbs together in a
large bowl. Stir in the chicken then remove
from the heat. Stuff the cannelloni with the
chicken mixture. Pour half the sauce into a
23 x 33-cm/9 x 13-inch baking dish. Place
the stuffed cannelloni on top. Pour over the
remaining sauce. Sprinkle with the mozzarella
and cover with foil. Bake in a preheated oven,
180°C/350°F/Gas Mark 4, for 45 minutes.
Let the dish stand for 10 minutes before
garnishing with basil sprigs and serving.

# chicken lasagna

## ingredients

**SERVES 6**

2 tbsp olive oil

900 g/2 lb fresh minced
   chicken

1 garlic clove, finely chopped

4 carrots, chopped

4 leeks, sliced

450 ml/16 fl oz chicken stock

2 tbsp tomato purée

salt and pepper

115 g/4 oz Cheddar cheese,
   grated

1 tsp Dijon mustard

double quantity of béchamel
   sauce (see page 230)

115 g/4 oz dried no-precook
   lasagna

## method

**1** Heat the oil in a heavy-based saucepan.
Add the chicken and cook over medium heat,
breaking it up with a wooden spoon, for
5 minutes, or until it is browned all over. Add
the garlic, carrots and leeks to the pan and
cook, stirring occasionally, for 5 minutes.

**2** Stir in the chicken stock and tomato purée
and season with salt and pepper. Bring to the
boil, reduce the heat, cover and simmer for
30 minutes.

**3** Whisk half the cheese and the mustard into
the hot béchamel sauce. In a large ovenproof
dish, make alternate layers of the chicken
mixture, lasagna and cheese sauce, ending
with a layer of cheese sauce. Sprinkle with the
remaining cheese and bake in a preheated
oven, 190°C/375°F/Gas Mark 5, for 1 hour,
or until golden brown and bubbling. Serve
at once.

# marsala mushroom lasagna

## ingredients

**SERVES 4**

butter, for greasing

14 sheets dried no-precook lasagna

triple quantity of béchamel sauce (see page 230)

85 g/3 oz grated Parmesan cheese

### exotic mushroom sauce

2 tbsp olive oil

2 garlic cloves, crushed

1 large onion, finely chopped

225 g/8 oz exotic mushrooms, sliced

300 g/10½ oz fresh minced chicken

85 g/3 oz chicken livers, finely chopped

115 g/4 oz prosciutto, diced

150 ml/5 fl oz Marsala wine

285 g/10 oz canned chopped tomatoes

1 tbsp chopped fresh basil leaves

2 tbsp tomato purée

salt and pepper

## method

**1** To make the sauce, heat the olive oil in a large, heavy-based saucepan. Add the garlic, onion and mushrooms and cook, stirring frequently, for 6 minutes. Add the minced chicken, chicken livers and prosciutto and cook over low heat for 12 minutes, or until the meat has browned.

**2** Stir the Marsala, tomatoes, basil and tomato purée into the mixture, and cook for 4 minutes. Season with salt and pepper, cover and simmer for 30 minutes. Uncover, stir, then simmer for a further 15 minutes.

**3** Lightly grease an ovenproof dish with butter. Arrange sheets of lasagna over the base of the dish, spoon over a layer of the exotic mushroom sauce, then spoon over a layer of béchamel sauce. Place another layer of lasagna on top and repeat the process twice, finishing with a layer of béchamel sauce. Sprinkle over the grated cheese and bake in a preheated oven, 190°C/375°F/Gas Mark 5, for 35 minutes, or until golden brown and bubbling. Serve immediately.

# chicken & wild mushroom cannelloni

## ingredients

**SERVES 4**

butter, for greasing

2 tbsp olive oil

2 garlic cloves, crushed

1 large onion, finely chopped

225 g/8 oz wild mushrooms, sliced

350 g/12 oz minced chicken

115 g/4 oz prosciutto, diced

150 ml/5 fl oz Marsala wine

200 g/7 oz canned chopped tomatoes

1 tbsp shredded fresh basil leaves

2 tbsp tomato purée

salt and pepper

10–12 dried cannelloni tubes

double quantity of béchamel sauce (see page 230)

85 g/3 oz freshly grated Parmesan cheese

## method

**1** Lightly grease a large ovenproof dish. Heat the olive oil in a heavy-based frying pan. Add the garlic, onion and mushrooms and cook over low heat, stirring frequently, for 8–10 minutes. Add the minced chicken and prosciutto and cook, stirring frequently, for 12 minutes, or until browned all over. Stir in the Marsala, tomatoes and their can juices, basil and tomato purée and cook for 4 minutes. Season with salt and pepper, then cover and simmer for 30 minutes. Uncover, stir and simmer for 15 minutes.

**2** Meanwhile, bring a large, heavy-based saucepan of lightly salted water to the boil. Add the pasta, return to the boil and cook for 8–10 minutes, or until tender but still firm to the bite. Using a slotted spoon, transfer the pasta to a plate and pat dry with kitchen paper.

**3** Using a teaspoon, fill the cannelloni tubes with the chicken, prosciutto and mushroom mixture. Transfer them to the ovenproof dish. Pour the béchamel sauce over them to cover completely and sprinkle with the grated Parmesan cheese.

**4** Bake the cannelloni in a preheated oven, 190°C/375°F/Gas Mark 5, for 30 minutes, or until golden brown and bubbling. Serve at once.

# lasagna alla marinara

## ingredients

**SERVES 6**

1 tbsp butter

225 g/8 oz raw prawns, shelled, deveined and coarsely chopped

450 g/1 lb monkfish fillets, skinned and chopped

225 g/8 oz chestnut mushrooms, chopped

triple quantity of béchamel sauce (see page 230)

salt and pepper

400 g/14 oz canned chopped tomatoes

1 tbsp chopped fresh chervil

1 tbsp shredded fresh basil

175 g/6 oz dried no-precook lasagna

85 g/3 oz freshly grated Parmesan cheese

## method

**1** Melt the butter in a large, heavy-based saucepan. Add the prawns and monkfish and cook over medium heat for 3–5 minutes, or until the prawns change colour. Transfer the prawns to a small heatproof bowl with a slotted spoon. Add the mushrooms to the pan and cook, stirring occasionally, for 5 minutes. Transfer the fish and mushrooms to the bowl.

**2** Stir the fish mixture, with any juices, into the béchamel sauce and season to taste with salt and pepper.

**3** Layer the tomatoes, chervil, basil, fish mixture and lasagna sheets in a large ovenproof dish, ending with a layer of the fish mixture. Sprinkle evenly with the grated Parmesan cheese. Bake in a preheated oven, 190°C/ 375°F/Gas Mark 5, for 35 minutes, or until golden brown, then serve immediately.

# baked tuna &
# ricotta rigatoni

## ingredients

**SERVES 4**

450 g/1 lb dried rigatoni
115 g/4 oz sun-dried
  tomatoes in oil, drained
  and sliced

### filling

200 g/7 oz canned flaked
  tuna, drained
225 g/8 oz ricotta cheese

### sauce

125 ml/4 fl oz double cream
225 g/8 oz freshly grated
  Parmesan cheese
salt and pepper

## method

**1** Lightly grease a large ovenproof dish with butter. Bring a large, heavy-based saucepan of lightly salted water to the boil. Add the rigatoni, return to the boil and cook for 8–10 minutes, or until just tender but still firm to the bite. Drain the pasta and let stand until cool enough to handle.

**2** Meanwhile, mix the tuna and ricotta cheese together in a bowl to form a soft paste. Spoon the mixture into a pastry bag and use to fill the rigatoni. Arrange the filled pasta tubes side by side in the prepared dish.

**3** To make the sauce, mix the cream and Parmesan cheese together in a bowl and season with salt and pepper. Spoon the sauce over the rigatoni and top with the sun-dried tomatoes, arranged in a criss-cross pattern. Bake in a preheated oven, 200°C/400°F/Gas Mark 6, for 20 minutes. Serve hot straight from the dish.

# layered spaghetti with smoked salmon & prawns

## ingredients

**SERVES 6**

350 g/12 oz dried spaghetti

70 g/2¹/₂ oz butter, plus extra
for greasing

200 g/7 oz smoked salmon,
cut into strips

280 g/10 oz jumbo prawns,
cooked, shelled
and deveined

300 ml/10 fl oz béchamel
sauce (see page 230)

115 g/4 oz freshly grated
Parmesan cheese

## method

**1** Bring a large saucepan of lightly salted water to the boil. Add the pasta, return to the boil and cook for 8–10 minutes, or until tender but still firm to the bite. Drain well, return to the pan, add 4 tablespoons of the butter and toss well.

**2** Spoon half the spaghetti into a large, greased ovenproof dish, cover with the strips of smoked salmon, then top with the prawns. Pour over half the béchamel sauce and sprinkle with half the Parmesan. Add the remaining spaghetti, cover with the remaining sauce and sprinkle with the remaining Parmesan. Dice the remaining butter and dot it over the surface.

**3** Bake in a preheated oven, 180°C/350°F/ Gas Mark 4, for 15 minutes, or until the top is golden brown. Serve immediately.

# tuna noodle casserole

## ingredients

### SERVES 2

125–150 g/4$^1$/$_2$–5$^1$/$_2$ oz
    dried macaroni

1 tbsp olive oil

1 garlic clove, crushed

55 g/2 oz white mushrooms,
    sliced

$^1$/$_2$ red pepper, thinly sliced

200 g/7 oz canned tuna in
    spring water, drained
    and flaked

$^1$/$_2$ tsp dried oregano

salt and pepper

2 tomatoes, sliced

2 tbsp dried breadcrumbs

25 g/1 oz grated mature
    Cheddar or Parmesan
    cheese

### sauce

2 tbsp butter, plus extra
    for greasing

1 tbsp plain flour

250 ml/8 fl oz milk

## method

**1** Bring a large saucepan of lightly salted water to the boil. Add the macaroni, return to the boil and cook for 10–12 minutes, or until tender but still firm to the bite. Drain, rinse and drain again thoroughly.

**2** Heat the olive oil in a frying pan and cook the garlic, mushrooms and pepper until soft. Add the tuna, oregano and salt and pepper. Heat through. Grease a 1-litre/32-fl oz ovenproof dish with a little butter or margarine. Add half of the cooked macaroni, cover with the tuna mixture, then add the remaining macaroni.

**3** To make the sauce, melt the butter in a pan, stir in the flour and cook for 1 minute. Gradually add the milk and bring to the boil. Simmer for 1–2 minutes, stirring constantly, until thickened. Season with salt and pepper. Pour the sauce over the macaroni. Lay the sliced tomatoes over the sauce and sprinkle with the breadcrumbs and cheese. Cook in a preheated oven, 200°C/400°F/Gas Mark 6, for 25 minutes, or until piping hot and the top is well browned.

# shellfish casserole

## ingredients

### SERVES 6

350 g/12 oz dried conchiglie

6 tbsp butter, plus extra
for greasing

2 fennel bulbs, thinly sliced

175 g/6 oz mushrooms,
thinly sliced

175 g/6 oz cooked shelled
prawns

175 g/6 oz cooked crabmeat

pinch of cayenne pepper

300 ml/10 fl oz béchamel
sauce (see page 230)

55 g/2 oz freshly grated
Parmesan cheese

2 beefsteak tomatoes, sliced

olive oil, for brushing

green salad and crusty bread,
to serve

## method

**1** Bring a large, heavy-based saucepan of lightly salted water to the boil. Add the pasta, return to the boil and cook for 8–10 minutes, or until tender but still firm to the bite. Drain well, return to the pan and stir in 2 tablespoons of the butter. Cover the pan and keep warm.

**2** Meanwhile, melt the remaining butter in a large, heavy-based frying pan. Add the fennel and cook over medium heat for 5 minutes, or until softened. Stir in the mushrooms and cook for a further 2 minutes. Stir in the prawns and crabmeat and cook for a further 1 minute, then remove the skillet from the heat.

**3** Grease 6 small ovenproof dishes with butter. Stir the cayenne pepper into the béchamel sauce, add the shellfish mixture and pasta, then spoon into the prepared dishes. Sprinkle with the Parmesan cheese and arrange the tomato slices on top, then brush the tomatoes with a little olive oil.

**4** Bake in a preheated oven, 180°C/350°F/Gas Mark 4, for 25 minutes, or until golden brown. Serve hot with a green salad and crusty bread.

# macaroni cheese

## ingredients

**SERVES 4**

225 g/8 oz macaroni

double quantity béchamel
sauce (see page 230)

1 egg, beaten

125 g/4$^1$/$_2$ oz mature Cheddar
cheese, grated

1 tbsp wholegrain mustard

2 tbsp chopped fresh chives

salt and pepper

4 tomatoes, sliced

125 g/4$^1$/$_2$ oz Red Leicester
cheese, grated

60 g/2$^1$/$_4$ oz blue cheese, grated

2 tbsp sunflower seeds

snipped fresh chives,
to garnish

## method

**1** Bring a large saucepan of lightly salted water to the boil and cook the macaroni for 8–10 minutes, or until just tender. Drain well and place in an ovenproof dish.

**2** Stir the beaten egg, Cheddar cheese, mustard and chives into the béchamel sauce and season with salt and pepper. Spoon the mixture over the macaroni, making sure it is well covered. Top with a layer of the sliced tomatoes.

**3** Sprinkle the Red Leicester cheese, blue cheese and sunflower seeds over the top. Place on a baking sheet and bake in a preheated oven, 190°C/375°F/Gas Mark 5, for 25–30 minutes, or until bubbling and golden. Garnish with snipped fresh chives and serve at once.

# vegetarian lasagna

## ingredients

**SERVES 4**

olive oil, for brushing

2 aubergines, sliced

2 tbsp butter

1 garlic clove, finely chopped

4 courgettes, sliced

1 tbsp finely chopped fresh
flat-leaf parsley

1 tbsp finely chopped fresh
marjoram

225 g/8 oz mozzarella
cheese, grated

625 ml/20 fl oz strained
canned tomatoes

175 g/6 oz dried no-precook
lasagna

salt and pepper

béchamel sauce (see below)

55 g/2 oz freshly grated
Parmesan cheese

### béchamel sauce

300 ml/10 fl oz milk

1 bay leaf

6 black peppercorns

slice of onion

mace blade

2 tbsp butter

3 tbsp plain flour

salt and pepper

## method

**1** To make the béchamel sauce, pour the milk into a pan and add the bay leaf, peppercorns, onion and mace. Heat to just below boiling point, then remove from the heat, cover, infuse for 10 minutes and strain. Melt the butter in a separate pan. Sprinkle in the flour and cook over low heat, stirring constantly, for 1 minute. Gradually stir in the milk, then bring to the boil and cook, stirring, until thickened and smooth. Season with salt and pepper.

**2** Brush a griddle pan with olive oil and heat until smoking. Add half the aubergine slices and cook over medium heat for 8 minutes, or until golden brown all over. Remove from the griddle pan and drain on kitchen paper. Repeat with the remaining aubergine slices.

**3** Melt the butter in a frying pan and add the garlic, courgettes, parsley and marjoram. Cook over medium heat, stirring frequently, for 5 minutes, or until the courgettes are golden all over. Remove and drain on kitchen paper.

**4** Layer the aubergine, courgettes, mozzarella, strained tomatoes and lasagna in an ovenproof dish brushed with olive oil, seasoning as you go and finishing with a layer of lasagna. Pour over the béchamel sauce, sprinkle with the Parmesan cheese and bake in a preheated oven, 200°C/400°F/Gas Mark 6, for 30–40 minutes, or until golden brown. Serve at once.

# mixed vegetable agnolotti

## ingredients

**SERVES 4**

butter, for greasing

plain flour, for dusting

85 g/3 oz freshly grated
  Parmesan cheese

mixed salad leaves, to serve

### pasta dough

200 g/7 oz plain flour, plus
  extra for dusting

pinch of salt

2 eggs, lightly beaten

1 tbsp olive oil

### filling

125 ml/4 fl oz olive oil

1 red onion, chopped

3 garlic cloves, chopped

2 large aubergines,
  cut into chunks

3 large courgettes,
  cut into chunks

6 beefsteak tomatoes, peeled,
  deseeded and coarsely
  chopped

1 large green pepper,
  deseeded and diced

1 large red pepper, deseeded
  and diced

1 tbsp sun-dried tomato purée

1 tbsp shredded fresh basil

salt and pepper

## method

**1** To make the pasta dough, sift the flour into a food processor. Add the salt, eggs and olive oil and process until the dough begins to come together. Knead on a lightly floured board until smooth. Cover and let rest for 30 minutes.

**2** To make the filling, heat the olive oil in a large, heavy-based saucepan. Add the onion and garlic and cook over low heat, stirring occasionally, for 5 minutes, or until softened. Add the aubergine, courgettes, tomatoes, green and red peppers, sun-dried tomato purée and basil. Season with salt and pepper, cover and simmer gently, stirring occasionally, for 20 minutes.

**3** Lightly grease an ovenproof dish with butter. Roll out the pasta dough on a lightly floured board and stamp out 7.5-cm/3-inch circles with a plain cutter. Place a spoonful of the vegetable filling on one side of each circle. Dampen the edges slightly and fold the pasta circles over, pressing together to seal.

**4** Bring a large pan of lightly salted water to the boil. Add the agnolotti, in batches if necessary, return to the boil and cook for 3–4 minutes. Remove with a slotted spoon, drain and transfer to the dish. Sprinkle with the Parmesan cheese and bake in a preheated oven, 200°C/400°F/Gas Mark 6, for 20 minutes. Serve with salad leaves.

# baked pasta
# with mushrooms

## ingredients

**SERVES 4**

140 g/5 oz fontina cheese,
   thinly sliced

300 ml/10 fl oz béchamel
   sauce (see page 230)

6 tbsp butter, plus extra for
   greasing

350 g/12 oz mixed wild
   mushrooms, sliced

350 g/12 oz dried tagliatelle

2 egg yolks

salt and pepper

4 tbsp freshly grated romano
   cheese

mixed salad leaves, to serve

## method

**1** Stir the fontina cheese into the béchamel sauce and set aside.

**2** Melt 2 tablespoons of the butter in a large saucepan. Add the mushrooms and cook over low heat, stirring occasionally, for 10 minutes.

**3** Meanwhile, bring a large saucepan of lightly salted water to the boil. Add the pasta, return to the boil and cook for 8–10 minutes, or until tender but still firm to the bite. Drain, return to the pan and add the remaining butter, the egg yolks and about one third of the sauce, then season with salt and pepper. Toss well to mix, then gently stir in the mushrooms.

**4** Lightly grease a large, ovenproof dish with butter and spoon in the pasta mixture. Pour over the remaining sauce evenly and sprinkle with the grated romano cheese. Bake in a preheated oven, 200°C/400°F/Gas Mark 6, for 15–20 minutes, or until golden brown. Serve immediately with mixed salad leaves.

# mushroom cannelloni

## ingredients

**SERVES 4**

12 dried cannelloni tubes

2 tbsp butter

450 g/1 lb mixed wild
mushrooms, finely chopped

1 garlic clove, finely chopped

85 g/3 oz fresh breadcrumbs

150 ml/5 fl oz milk

4 tbsp olive oil, plus extra
for brushing

225 g/8 oz ricotta cheese

6 tbsp freshly grated
Parmesan cheese

salt and pepper

2 tbsp pine nuts

2 tbsp slivered almonds

### tomato sauce

2 tbsp olive oil

1 onion, finely chopped

1 garlic clove, finely chopped

800 g/1 lb 12 oz canned
chopped tomatoes

1 tbsp tomato purée

8 black olives, pitted
and chopped

salt and pepper

## method

**1** Bring a large saucepan of lightly salted water to the boil. Add the cannelloni tubes, return to the boil and cook for 8–10 minutes, or until tender but still firm to the bite. With a slotted spoon, transfer the tubes to a plate and pat dry.

**2** Meanwhile, make the tomato sauce. Heat the olive oil in a frying pan. Add the onion and garlic and cook over low heat for 5 minutes, or until softened. Add the tomatoes and their can juices, tomato purée and olives and season with salt and pepper. Bring to the boil and cook for 3–4 minutes. Pour the sauce into an large ovenproof dish brushed with olive oil.

**3** To make the filling, melt the butter in a heavy-based frying pan. Add the mushrooms and garlic and cook over medium heat, stirring frequently, for 3–5 minutes, or until tender. Remove the frying pan from the heat. Mix the breadcrumbs, milk and olive oil together in a large bowl, then stir in the ricotta, mushroom mixture and 4 tablespoons of the Parmesan cheese. Season with salt and pepper.

**4** Fill the cannelloni tubes with the mushroom mixture and place them in the dish. Brush with olive oil and sprinkle with the remaining Parmesan cheese, pine nuts and almonds. Bake in a preheated oven, 190°C/375°F/Gas Mark 5, for 25 minutes, or until golden.

# cannelloni with spinach & ricotta

## ingredients

**SERVES 4**

12 dried cannelloni tubes,
    7.5 cm/3 inches long

butter, for greasing

### filling

140 g/5 oz cooked lean ham,
    chopped

140 g/5 oz frozen spinach,
    thawed and drained

115 g/4 oz ricotta cheese

1 egg

3 tbsp freshly grated romano
    cheese

pinch of freshly grated nutmeg

salt and pepper

### cheese sauce

2 tbsp unsalted butter

2 tbsp plain flour

625 ml/20 fl oz hot milk

85 g/3 oz freshly grated
    Gruyère cheese

salt and pepper

## method

**1** Bring a large saucepan of lightly salted water to the boil. Add the cannelloni tubes, return to the boil and cook for 6–7 minutes, or until nearly tender. Drain and rinse under cold water. Spread out the tubes on a clean tea towel.

**2** Process the ham, spinach and ricotta in a food processor for a few seconds until combined. Add the egg and romano cheese and process again to a smooth paste. Transfer to a bowl and season with nutmeg, salt and pepper.

**3** Grease an ovenproof dish with butter. Spoon the filling into a pastry bag fitted with a 1-cm/ 1/2-inch tip. Carefully pipe the filling into the cannelloni tubes and place in the dish.

**4** To make the cheese sauce, melt the butter in a saucepan. Add the flour and cook over low heat, stirring constantly, for 1 minute. Gradually stir in the hot milk then bring to the boil, stirring constantly. Simmer over the lowest possible heat, stirring frequently, for 10 minutes until thickened and smooth. Remove the pan from the heat, stir in the Gruyère cheese and season with salt and pepper.

**5** Spoon the cheese sauce over the filled cannelloni. Cover the dish with foil and bake in a preheated oven, 180°C/350°F/Gas Mark 4, for 20–25 minutes. Serve immediately.